How to Use

Microsoft® Publisher 98

Rebecca Reese

SAMS

A Division of Macmillan Computer Publishing, USA
201 W. 103rd Street
Indianapolis, Indiana 46290

Contents at a Glance

How to Use Microsoft® Publisher 98

International Standard Book Number: 0-7897-1666-6

Library of Congress Catalog Card Number: **98-85821**

01 00 99 98   4   3   2   1

Interpretation of the printing code: the rightmost double-digit number is the year of the book's printing; the rightmost single-digit, the number of the book's printing. For example, a printing code of 98-1 shows that the first printing of the book occurred in 1998.

Composed in Rotis Semi Sans by Macmillan Computer Publishing

Printed in the United States of America

Executive Editor
Mark Taber

Acquisitions Editor
Randi Roger

Development Editor
Randi Roger

Managing Editor
Patrick Kanouse

Project Editor
Rebecca Mounts

Copy Editor
Tonya Maddox

Indexer
Kelly Talbot

Technical Reviewer
Ned Snell

Cover Designers
Nathan Clement
Aren Howell
Gary Adair

Book Designers
Nathan Clement
Ruth Harvey

Production
Carol Bowers
Ayanna Lacey
Gene Redding

Orders, Catalogs, and Customer Service

To order other Sams or Macmillan Computer Publishing books, catalogs, or products, please contact our Customer Service Department:

Phone: 1-800-428-5331

Fax: 1-800-882-8583

International Fax: 1-317-228-4400

Or visit our online bookstore:

`http://www.mcp.com/`

Contents

How to Use This Book

The Complete Visual Reference

Each chapter of this book is made up of a series of short, instructional tasks, designed to help you understand all the information that you need to get the most out of your computer hardware and software.

 Click: Click the left mouse button once.

 Double-click: Click the left mouse button twice in rapid succession.

 Right-click: Click the right mouse button once.

 Selection: Highlights the area onscreen discussed in the step or task.

 Key icons: Clearly indicate what key combinations to use.

Each task includes a series of easy-to-understand steps designed to guide you through the procedure.

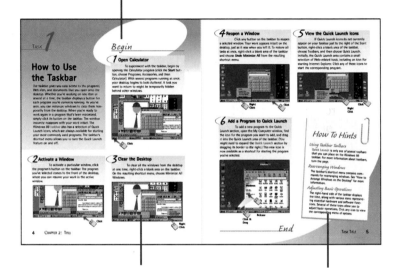

Each step is fully illustrated to show you how it looks onscreen.

Extra hints that tell you how to accomplish a goal are provided in most tasks.

Screen elements (such as dialog boxes, menus, icons, windows, and so on) as well as things you enter or select appear in **boldface**. Primary elements (graphics, for example) are also boldface.

Continues

If you see this symbol, it means the task you're in continues on the next page.

Introduction

*P*ublisher 98 is a desktop-publishing application, a unique and powerful software genre. You can use Publisher to create professional-looking publications without having to learn all the skills and jargon of the printing trade.

What is terrific about choosing Publisher 98 for your desktop-publishing chores is the amount of assistance built into the software. It's like having your own design team, including layout specialists, artists, and printing experts.

Wizards inhabit this software, and they show up for work at your beck and call. They walk you through the process of creating any of the numerous preconfigured publications:

- ✓ Newsletters
- ✓ Brochures
- ✓ Greeting cards
- ✓ Business stationery
- ✓ Banners
- ✓ Paper airplanes

How to Use Microsoft Publisher 98, Second Edition is written so that you get the most out of the wizards. You travel with the wizards throughout this book in short, simple, steps; you're then taken through all the additional steps necessary to turn the wizard's preconfigured layout into your own, personalized publication.

But you don't stop there. After you've created a few publications with the wizards, you'll want to strike out on your own. This book is aimed at getting you comfortable enough to make that daunting decision. You learn how to use all of Publisher 98's tools and features.

Some projects are included for you to complete. Even though they're fun to do, they're also a learning experience. You put the skills presented in this book to work when working on these projects.

Feel free to read this book in whatever order you choose. *How to Use Microsoft Publisher 98, Second Edition* isn't written with the thought that you'll read the pages and look at the illustrations starting with the first page and ending with the last. You can check the index to find the things you need to learn about.

In this book you find a no-nonsense approach to learning how to perform a task, complete with illustrations, which add to your learning experience.

Task

1

Getting Started

*B*efore you can dive into Publisher to publish a newspaper, a book, or a birthday card for Aunt Maude, you have to install the software. Then, of course, it's a good idea to learn your way around Publisher.

Even though Publisher looks and behaves in a fashion that's similar to other Windows software you may be familiar with, there are some differences you have to get used to.

Publisher is a graphics program with robust text functions (unlike most other desktop-publishing software, where text creation is onerous and you always find it easier to import text). As a result, you find more toolbars, more buttons on the toolbars, and a slew of menu commands that are unique to Publisher (and therefore new to you).

In this chapter you learn about installing, starting, and using Publisher features. You learn how to get help as you work. You also meet the all-powerful wizard that makes creating a complicated publication a snap. ●

How to Install Publisher

Before you can work and have fun in Publisher (it is a lot of fun), you have to install it. This is an easy procedure, but first you should close any software programs that may be open.

If you use a virus-checking program, you must disable it before beginning the installation. (You can start it again after Publisher 98 is installed.)

Begin

1 Put the CD-ROM in Its Drive

Most of the time, the Publisher 98 setup process starts automatically as soon as you put the CD-ROM in its drive (that's called AutoPlay). Choose **Continue** after you've read the text in the welcoming message.

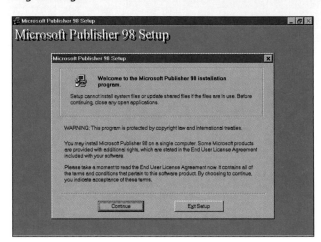

2 Starting Setup Manually

If AutoPlay doesn't start the setup process, click the **Start** button and choose **Run** from the **Start** menu. When the **Run** dialog box opens, enter **d:\setup** (assuming d: is the drive letter for your CD-ROM—if not, substitute the appropriate drive letter). The opening setup window appears.

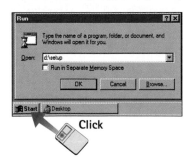

Click

3 Enter the Serial Number

Enter the CD key for your copy of Publisher 98; it's on an orange sticker on the back of the CD case. Choose **OK**. A dialog box shows your product ID number. Choose **OK** to move on.

4 Select the Publisher Folder

Publisher selects a folder into which the software will be installed. You can choose **Change Folder** to change the destination folder if you want to (a folder will be created automatically if you enter one that doesn't exist). Choose **OK**.

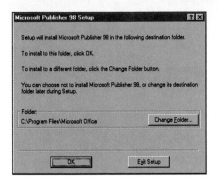

5 Accept the License

Use the scrollbar to read through the License Agreement and then choose **I Agree**. If you don't agree, installation stops.

6 Choose the Type of Installation

Setup spends a few seconds looking for previously installed versions of Publisher, and then the **Setup** dialog box asks you which type of installation you want to perform. Choose **Typical Installation**. The only real difference is that the **Custom Installation** permits you to load all the clip art onto your hard drive, which is not a good idea—it uses many millions of bytes. It's better to access the clip art from the CD-ROM.

7 Wait for Notification of Success

It takes a few moments to copy all the files to your hard drive. Publisher then lets you know that the setup procedure worked.

End

How to Start Publisher

Before you dive in to produce a book, newspaper, greeting card, or business stationery, it's a good idea to familiarize yourself with opening and closing Publisher 98, as well as the software window.

Begin

1 Open the Start Menu

Choose **Programs**, Microsoft Publisher 98 from the **Start** menu.

Click

2 Welcome to Publisher

The first time you use Publisher 98, a Welcome message greets you. You can choose to view one of the Publisher demos or opt to begin using the software immediately. (Clicking the **Done** button is the same as choosing **Start using Publisher now**.)

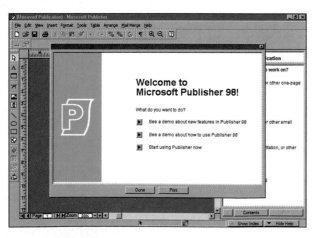

3 Introducing the Catalog

The **Publisher Catalog** opens so you can get right to work. This Catalog is the first thing you see every time you start Publisher 98. Information about using the Catalog is found throughout this book, so it's not discussed here. For now, choose **Exit Catalog**.

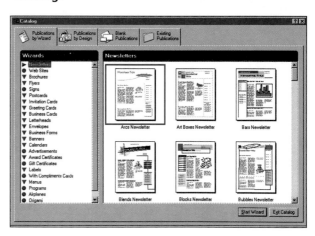

4 Examining the Publisher Window

The **Publisher** window looks very much like all the Windows software you use.

Title bar   Menu bar   Standard toolbar

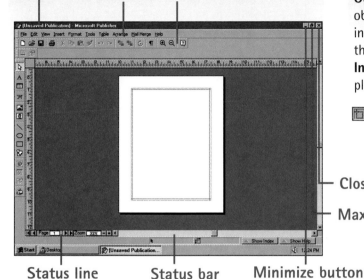

Close button

Maximize/Restore button

Status line   Status bar   Minimize button

5 The Status Bar Is Special

The **Publisher** status bar is unique (compared to most other Windows software). It has four elements. The **Object Position** indicator and the **Object Size** indicator are related to any selected object—if no object is selected, the **Object Position** indicator displays the mouse pointer's position and the **Object Size** indicator is empty. The **Show/Hide Index** button and the **Show/Hide Help** (which displays Help pages) button are also on the status bar.

6 Closing Publisher

To close Publisher, click the **Close** button (the **X** in the upper-right corner) or choose **File**, **Exit** from the **menu bar**. If you have made any changes to your publication since you last saved it, you're given a chance to save it again before the software shuts down.

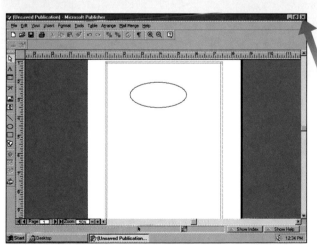

Click

How-To Hints

Make a Desktop Shortcut

Create a desktop shortcut in order to make it easier to launch Publisher. Open Explorer and find the file named **Mspub.exe**. Right-drag its icon to the desktop. When you release the mouse, choose **Create Shortcut(s) Here** from the displayed menu, and then just double-click the shortcut to open Publisher.

End

How to Choose a Publication Wizard

The easiest way to design a publication is to let a wizard do the preliminary work. That means the layout, color design, and other setup options are configured automatically and all you have to worry about is writing the text (which, by the way, isn't a cakewalk).

The wizards reside in the Catalog, which is the first thing you see when you open Publisher 98.

Begin

1 Use the Menu Bar

If you're already working in Publisher, choose **File**, **New** from the **menu bar**. Don't click the **New** icon on the toolbar, and don't use the **Ctrl+N** shortcut—neither of them brings up the Catalog (you'll only get a blank page).

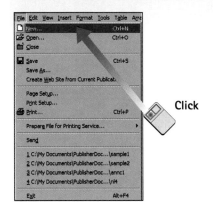

Click

2 Choose a Wizard and a Style

On the **Publications by Wizard** tab of the Catalog, a list of wizards displays on the left side of the window. When you select a wizard, its set of publications displays on the right side of the window. Most wizards have quite a few publication styles to offer, and you can use the scrollbar to examine all of them.

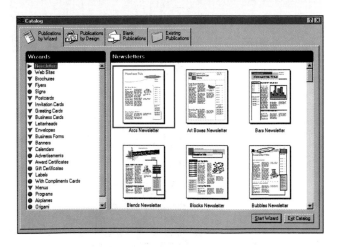

3 Understanding the Wizard

Wizards with a circle next to the name offer a single publication type. Wizards with a downward-facing arrow symbol have multiple publications. The list expands when you click the arrow (click again to close the list). The selected wizard displays a right-facing arrow, regardless of its original symbol.

4 Choosing a Special Paper Wizard

Wizards that are named **Special Paper** display publication types that include the logo for a company named PaperDirect. Information about purchasing this paper is found in the PaperDirect catalog included in your Publisher package. The color design for PaperDirect is built into the paper; you don't have to add it graphically. This means you don't have to have a color printer to have color in your publication.

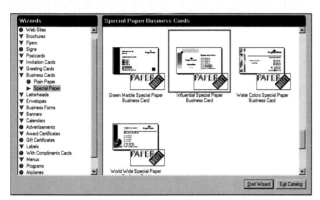

5 Start the Wizard

After you've selected a wizard and a publication type, choose **Start Wizard** to begin the process of building the publication.

6 Closing the Catalog

If you decide you don't want to use any wizard for this publication, you can close the Catalog by choosing **Exit Catalog** (or click the **X** in the upper-right corner of the Catalog window).

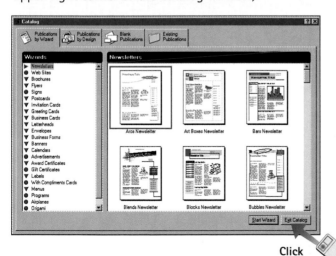

Click

How-To Hints

Eliminating the Catalog

After you've become an expert in Publisher (with the help of this book), you can eliminate the Catalog display when you open the software. Choose Tools, Options from the menu bar and check the box for the option called Use Catalog at startup. Checking the box removes the check mark, and hereafter the Catalog won't load automatically on startup.

End

Working with the Publication Wizard

The wizard does a lot of work, but you can direct its efforts with your own preferences. The first preference, of course, is selecting the publication and style of publication. Then there are other decisions for you to make; the wizard makes adjustments to the publication as you make your decisions.

Begin

1 Launch the Wizard

After you select a publication type, choose **Start Wizard**; this tells the wizard to begin putting your publication together. The wizard starts building the layout, which is based on the publication and style you selected.

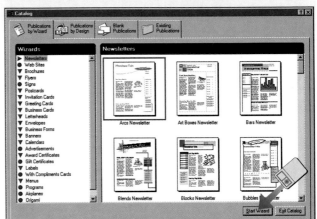

Click

2 Begin the Wizard's Questions

When the **wizard** pane opens on the left side of the screen, the wizard is ready to start. Click **Next** to begin selecting configuration options.

3 Answer Each Question

The questions vary, depending on the type of publication you selected. For instance, the **Newsletter Wizard** wants to know about columns, mailing labels, and whether you plan to print on both sides of the paper. Continue to make selections, choosing **Next** to move on.

4 Choose Finish

The **Next** button is grayed out when you have answered the last query. Choose **Finish**.

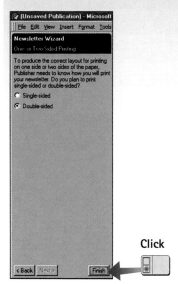

Click

5 You Can Change Your Mind

The **wizard** pane displays the question categories. To change any of your decisions, click the appropriate category; you're returned to that wizard page to make the necessary changes.

6 Hide the Wizard

To have the use of your entire **Publisher** window, choose **Hide Wizard**. The **wizard** pane disappears. If you want to revisit your decisions, choose **Show Wizard** to bring back the pane shown in Step 5.

How-To Hints

Jumping to the Final Wizard Pane

You can perform a shortcut after becoming familiar with working with wizards: You can choose **Finish** as soon as the first wizard pane appears and move to the final **wizard** pane (with the list of categories displayed so you can make changes to the design). If you choose this shortcut, Publisher 98 asks you to confirm it and also inquires whether you'd like to make this a habit.

End

How to Choose a Design Set

The Publisher Catalog has a tab named **Publications by Design**. The preformatted publication layouts available in this tab are *design sets*, which means they share a common design. You can use these design sets to create a variety of publication types, and all of them will share the same design elements (such as colors, fonts, and overall style). This is a great way to create matching business stationery and forms.

Begin

1 Opening the Catalog

If you're already working in Publisher, choose **File**, **New** from the **menu bar** to open the Catalog. (The Catalog appears automatically if you're just starting Publisher.)

2 Move to the Designs Tab

Click the **Publications by Design** tab.

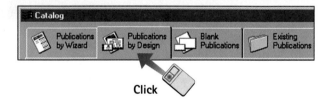

Click

3 Choose a Design Set

The Catalog's left pane contains a list of design sets, each of which can be expanded by clicking the down-facing arrow next to the name. When you expand a design set, the list of designs contained in that set is displayed.

4 View the Available Publications

Select a design in the left pane in order to display the available publications in the right pane.

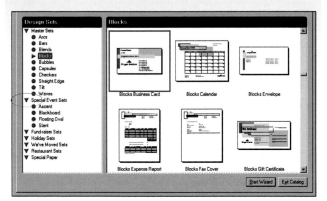

5 Select a Publication

Choose the publication you want to create by clicking its picture in the right pane, and then choose **Start Wizard**.

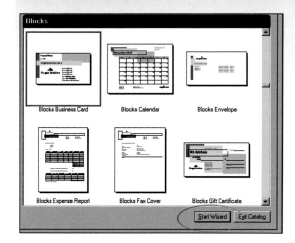

6 Answer the Wizard's Questions

Choose **Next** in the **wizard** pane to move from window to window, answering the wizard's questions. When you get to the last wizard window, the **Next** button is grayed out. Choose **Finish**. The wizard displays the list of option windows, and you can choose the appropriate one if you want to change any of your decisions.

How-To Hints

Hide the Wizard

It's easier to work in the **Publisher** window if you hide the wizard by clicking the **Hide Wizard** button (which is found on the bottom of the **wizard** pane). If you want to make changes to the design, click **Show Wizard** to bring back the **wizard** pane shown in Step 6.

End

How to Use a Blank Publication Design

The Publisher Catalog offers a host of designs and layouts in the **Blank Publications** tab. These are commonly used for publications you want to create from scratch, but you're limited to a particular paper size, or some paper-folding pattern.

Begin

1 Open the Catalog

If you're already working in Publisher, choose **File**, **New** from the **menu bar** to open the Catalog. (If you're just starting Publisher, the Catalog appears automatically.)

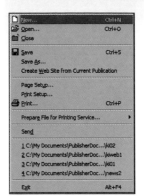

2 Select the Blank Publications Tab

Click the **Blank Publications** tab at the top of the **Catalog** window.

Click

3 Choose a Publication

Select a publication type. You can either click its name in the left pane or click its picture in the right pane.

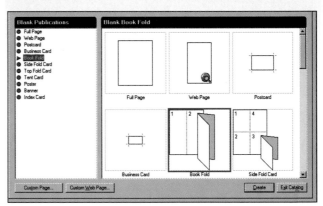

4 Design a Custom Page

If the paper size or folding pattern you need isn't available, choose **Custom Page**.

Click

5 Select a Custom Layout

In the **Page Setup** dialog box, choose the layout type you need from the top section of the dialog box. The bottom section of the dialog box changes to reflect your selection's options. Make changes to the specifications at the bottom of the dialog box as needed.

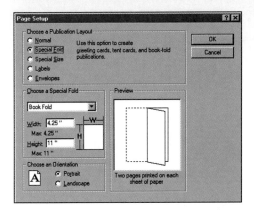

6 Labels Are Supported Too

If you choose **Labels** as the publication type, the dialog box displays the full range of labels available from Avery. Select the one you plan to use, and Publisher displays a page that's laid out to match the Labels page.

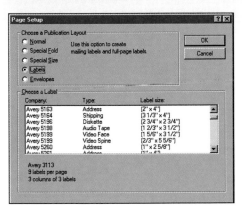

How-To Hints

Printing Labels

When you use labels in a laser printer, it's a good idea to send them through the printer in a straight path (you may have to flip down a back door to generate the straight-path feeding mode). Labels sometimes peel if they go around the roller. In addition, never put a label page back through the printer for a second run—you run the risk of destroying the printer's mechanism. If you don't use all the labels on a page, throw the page away anyway.

End

How to Create a Publication from Scratch

Publisher offers all sorts of opportunities to use preformatted layouts, but after you're comfortable with all the Publisher features and tools, you're likely to want to try working without a net.

Starting with a blank page can be a bit intimidating because there aren't any preset frames or margins, but with some careful planning you can create a publication just as slick and professional as the predesigned templates.

Begin

1 Close the Catalog

To get to a blank page when you first launch Publisher, click the **Exit Catalog** button, which is at the bottom of the **Catalog** window.

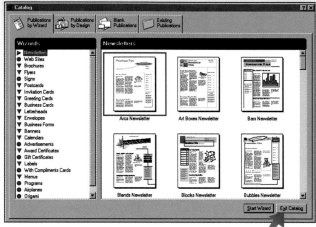

Click

2 Use the New Icon

If you're already working in Publisher, you can open a blank page by clicking the **New** icon on the **Standard** toolbar (or by pressing **Ctrl+N**).

3 Open the Page Setup Dialog Box

Because you don't have a predefined page layout, you must set up your page manually. Choose **File**, **Page Setup**.

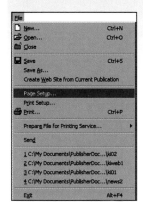

4 Configure the Page

Use the options in the **Page Setup** dialog box to configure the page size, along with any other options you need for this publication. Click **OK** to save your choices.

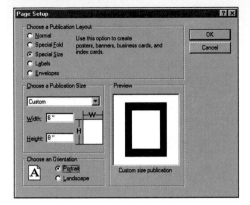

5 Configure the Layout

To establish margins and other layout options, choose **Arrange**, **Layout Guides** from the **menu bar**. When the **Layout Guides** dialog box appears, specify the margins you need and insert columns and rows if you require them. See Chapter 2, Task 7, "How to Create Columns in Text Frames," for more information about using this dialog box.

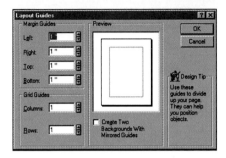

6 Add the Elements

Now you're ready to create a masterpiece. Add text frames, pictures, and other elements to your page as described throughout this book.

How-To Hints

About Page Sizes

If you create a page layout of a custom size, Publisher assumes you'll print it on standard size paper. If you have paper that matches your layout's size, you must tell the printer about it by using the **File**, **Print Setup** command.

End

How to Navigate Through a Publication

Working with Publisher is a bit different from working with your word processor. You can't use the scrollbar to move from the first page to any additional pages.

Because Publisher is a desktop publishing application, it's important to see a full-page view—that way you can keep an eye on the layout. Each page in a publication is an individual object and is brought into the window by itself. However, if you're printing on both sides of the paper and your publication will be bound like a book, you can also view a two-page spread.

Begin

1 Use the Page Controls

The page controls below the document window are the tools you use to move through your publication's pages. Move to the first page quickly by clicking the **First Page** arrow (which is a left-facing arrow with a vertical line). Move just as rapidly to the last page by clicking the **Last Page** arrow, which is the rightmost arrow on the page controls (a right-facing arrow with a vertical line).

2 Move to the Adjacent Page

Use the arrows that are next to the box with the current page to move to the previous or next page.

3 Move to a Specific Page

Click the box that displays the current page to open the **Go To Page** dialog box. Enter the page number you want to go to. Press **OK** to see that page in the **Publisher** window.

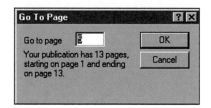

④ View Double Pages

To see adjacent pages the way they will print, choose **View, Two-Page Spread** from the **menu bar**. This command is a toggle, and when you want to return to a single-page view, select it again to remove the check mark.

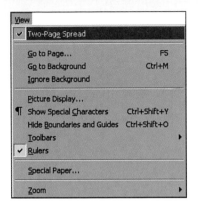

⑤ Zoom In and Out

To zoom in (helpful when you're working in a frame) or zoom out (to see the overall layout), click the box with the current zoom percentage; then choose a zoom mode from the pop-up menu.

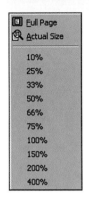

⑥ Quick Zoom

Use the **plus** and **minus** keys that are to the right of the current percentage box to zoom in and out in graduated steps. Each time you click, the zoom percentage changes in a pattern that matches the zoom percentages shown in Step 5. For instance, click the plus sign to move from **33%** to **50%**.

End

How-To Hints

About Two-Page Spreads

When you view a two-page spread, the odd page is always on the right and the even page is on the left. This means that if you move to the first or last page of your publication, only one page will display. Page 1 has nothing to the left of it, and the last page (which is an even numbered page) has nothing to the right.

How to Add and Remove Pages

If you are creating a publication from scratch, you start with a single blank page and then you must add pages as you need them. Even if you use a wizard design, however, you may find that the original layout didn't provide enough pages.

As you perfect your publication by editing the stories and resizing the frames, you may find it necessary to delete a page.

Begin

1 Add a Page at the End

If you're working on the last page of your publication and you have more to say, you can easily tack on a page at the end of the publication. Just click the **Next Page** button.

2 Reassure Publisher

Publisher wants to be sure that you didn't click the **Next Page** button in error, and asks if you want to add a page. Click **OK** to add the page. Publisher displays the new page in the window so you can go right to work on it.

3 Insert a Page Within the Publication

If you need to insert a page anywhere in the publication, move to the page either immediately before or immediately after the new page location; then choose **Insert**, **Page** from the **menu bar**.

4 Specify the New Page Options

Specify the options you need for the new page in the **Insert Page** dialog box.

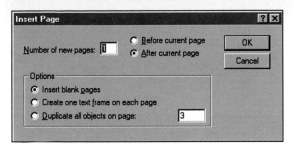

5 Adding Two Pages at a Time

If you're working with a **Two-Page Spread** view of your publication, Publisher understands that you need to add two pages at a time to make sure your publication can be bound or folded correctly. The **Insert Page** dialog box makes the proper adjustments in the options offered. If you specify an odd number of new pages, Publisher issues a warning (but doesn't stop you).

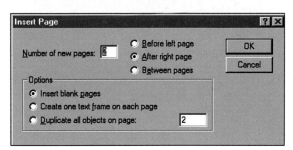

6 Deleting Pages

If you want to delete a page, be sure that page is in the **Publisher** window and choose **Edit**, **Delete Page**—the page disappears. If you are working in the **Two-Page Spread** view, the **Delete Page** dialog box appears and offers a default option of deleting both pages (to keep your publication pages at an even number). Choose the option you need and click **OK**.

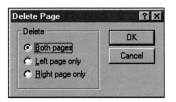

How-To Hints

Keep Two-Page Publications Even

If you ignore Publisher's recommendation to delete two pages at a time from a publication that you're going to bind or fold, add another page somewhere else.

End

TASK *10*

How to Use the Standard Toolbar

Working with the menu system can be tedious because you have to click the menu item, position your mouse just so over a command, and then click again to invoke the command. If there's a submenu, you have to position your mouse a second time and then click.

To make life easier (your life in Publisher at least), the commonly used menu commands have been placed on buttons (also called *icons*) on a toolbar called the **Standard** toolbar. It sits right below your **menu bar**.

One click on an icon produces the same result as going through the menu system. It's amazing how many people never really take a careful look at this toolbar to see what it offers, and therefore never use it. To make sure you don't fall in this category, let's go over the **Standard** toolbar buttons.

2 Print

Clicking the **Print** icon sends the publication to the printer with the last set of options you selected in the **Print** dialog box. If this is the first time you're printing in this Publisher session, your entire document is printed. No dialog box appears to ask you whether you want to change printers, print only specific pages, or make any other choices.

Begin

1 File Tools

The first three icons on the left edge of the **Standard** toolbar are for working with files (publications). From left to right the buttons are: **New**, which opens a new blank publication; **Open**, which brings up a dialog box from which you can select an existing publication to open; and **Save**, which saves your publication.

3 Move and Copy Elements

The next four buttons are used to move and copy your publication's contents. From left to right, they are: **Cut**, which removes the element (text, graphic, or the like) from your publication and places it on the Windows Clipboard; **Copy**, which places a copy of the element on the Windows Clipboard (but doesn't remove it from the publication); **Paste**, which inserts the contents of the Windows Clipboard in the location of your pointer when you click the **Paste** button; and **Format Painter**, which copies the formatting of a frame (rather than copying the elements in the frame) and then pastes that formatting on another frame. Of course, this means the **Format Painter** icon requires two separate clicks, one to copy and one to paste.

4 Oops!

Next in line are the **Undo** and **Redo** buttons. You can undo your last action, and after you do so, you can redo the previous undo if you change your mind again. If you can't remember what you did last (or undid last), hold your mouse pointer on either button to see a ScreenTip reminder.

6 Change the View

Use the next three buttons to change the way your publication looks in the window. The **Show Special Characters** button changes text frames so that each space, tab, and paragraph marker is displayed with special characters. To return to plain text, click the button again (that changes its name to **Hide Special Characters**). Click the **Zoom In** button and your pointer turns into a **magnifying glass** with a **plus sign**. Click anywhere on the current page to zoom in on that spot (your pointer then returns to normal). The **Zoom Out** button works in the opposite manner (the **magnifying glass** has a **minus sign**).

5 Manipulating Frames

Use the next three buttons to manipulate frames in your publication. **Bring to Front** moves the selected frame to the top of a set of layered frames. **Send to Back** moves the selected frame to the bottom of a pile of layered frames. Click **Custom Rotate** to open a dialog box that permits you to specify the number of degrees by which to rotate the frame. (The dialog box also has rotate arrows you can click to effect a manual rotation of the frame.) See Chapter 3, Task 5, "How to Layer Shapes," for more information on working with layers.

7 Summon the Office Assistant

The last button on the **Standard** toolbar looks like a **question mark**, and it's named **Microsoft Publisher Help**. However, it doesn't bring up the **Help** files—it calls the **Office Assistant**. See Task 17, "How to Use the Office Assistant," later in this chapter for more information.

End

How-To Hints

What Exactly Are ScreenTips?

Can't remember what all those icons on the toolbars stand for? ScreenTips take care of that! Just put your cursor on a button/icon and wait for the name of the button to appear.

Get Rid of ScreenTips

If you don't like these names popping up every time you move your cursor over the buttons/icons, feel free to turn off the ScreenTips. To do that, select **View, Toolbars, Options**. Click the **Show ScreenTips on Toolbars** box to add or remove the check mark. Click **OK**.

How to Use the Objects Toolbar

Everything you do in Publisher starts with a frame, and the frames you need are created with the **Objects** toolbar.

This toolbar is positioned vertically on the left side of your screen, but you can move it by placing your pointer on the ridge at the top of the toolbar and dragging it to a different location.

Begin

1 Pointer Tool

The first (topmost) button on the **Objects** toolbar is the **Pointer Tool** button. Click it when you need to have your mouse pointer work in its usual fashion instead of displaying a special pointer indicating some task that's in process. You can click anywhere in the **Publisher** window, outside the pages, to accomplish the same thing.

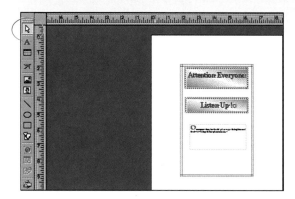

2 Text Frames

Use the **Text Frame Tool** and **Table Frame Tool** buttons to create plain text frames and table text frames.

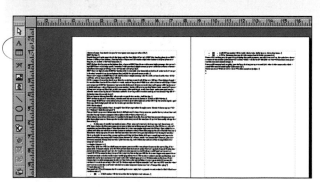

3 Graphic Frames

The next three buttons are for creating graphic frames. Use the **WordArt Frame Tool** button to create WordArt. The **Picture Frame Tool** button is used to insert a picture file, usually something you've scanned, downloaded, or received from a friend. The **Clip Gallery Tool** button is used to create a frame that holds clip art or other objects from the Microsoft Clip Gallery.

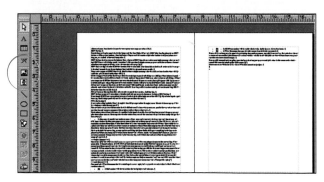

4 Shapes

The four **Shapes** buttons are: **Line Tool**, **Oval Tool** (also used for circles), **Rectangle Tool** (also used for squares), and **Custom Shapes**. Click any of the first three to create a standard shape. Click the **Custom Shapes** button to open a selection of shapes you can choose from.

5 Web Tools

The three Web tool buttons are only accessible when you're working on a Web publication (these buttons are grayed out for standard publications). The **Hot Spot Tool** button is used to create a spot on a graphic into which you insert a hyperlink. The **Form Control** button is used to create forms on your Web pages. The **HTML Code Fragment** button creates frames that hold HTML code. Information about all of these Web tools is found throughout Chapter 6, "Creating a Web Publication."

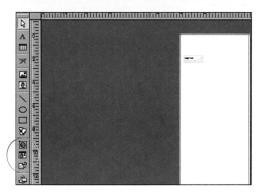

6 Standard Design Gallery

When you're working on a regular publication (as opposed to a Web publication), use the **Design Gallery Object** button to open the **Design Gallery** window. You find a host of special elements, including calendars, coupons, and tons of elaborate, professional designs you can use for headlines and attention-getters. Learn about using the Design Gallery in "How to Use the Design Gallery," which is Task 4 in Chapter 4.

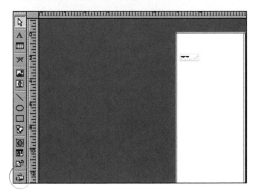

7 Web Design Gallery

Clicking the **Design Gallery Object** button when working on a Web publication brings up the Design Gallery; lots of objects that are designed specifically for Web pages are included.

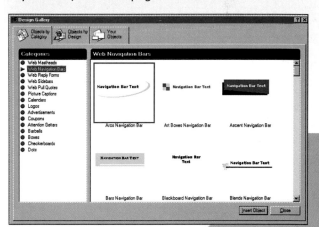

End

How to Use Layout Guides

Every publication you create must be designed and printed around a set of margins, which position the edge of the page. Otherwise, the edges of each page would fall in different places, or an element wouldn't print because it falls off the edge of the page.

In addition to the margins, you can establish imaginary (non-printing) lines on every page for use as alignment guides. In that case every element in your publication appears in a professionally aligned manner.

The margins and guide lines you set for your publication are called *layout guides*, and they affect every page.

Begin

1 Use the Layout Guides Command

To work with layout guides, choose **Arrange**, **Layout Guides** from the **menu bar**.

2 Set the Margins

In the **Layout Guides** dialog box, use the **Margin Guides** section to specify the margins you need for each side of the page. You can enter the numbers directly or use the **arrows** to change the defaults.

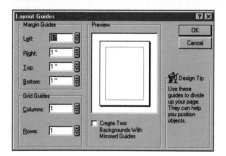

3 Set Vertical Guide Lines

If you need vertical alignment guides for the elements on your page(s), add **Columns** (one additional column for each vertical line you need). You can move these vertical lines to any position on the page after you close the dialog box.

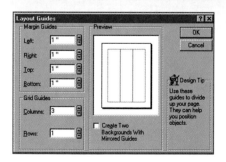

4 Set Horizontal Guide Lines

To use horizontal alignment guides, add more **Rows**. You can change the position of the guide lines after you close the dialog box.

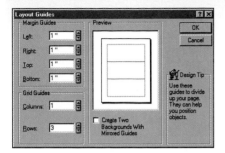

5 Create Mirrored Guide Lines

If your publication is going to be printed on both sides of the paper and then bound (binding can include staples), select the **Create Two Backgrounds With Mirrored Guides** option. Notice that the **Margin Guides** are now named **Inside** and **Outside**. Make sure the **Inside** margin specification allows enough room for your binding device. Choose **OK** to save your specifications and close the dialog box.

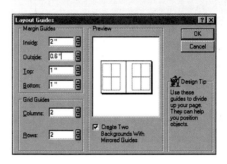

6 Adjust Guides to Fine-Tune the Layout

By default, layout guides divide your page into perfectly equal parts. To form a pleasing composition, you'll often want to move the guides so that the parts of the page are different sizes. Begin by choosing **View, Go to Background**. (See Chapter 4, Task 6, "How to Create Background Elements," to learn more about the background.) Hold the **Shift** key as you position your pointer over the line you want to move (the pointer turns into an **Adjust** pointer) and drag the line where you want it. When finished, choose **View, Go to Foreground** to return to the foreground and work with the text and graphics on the page.

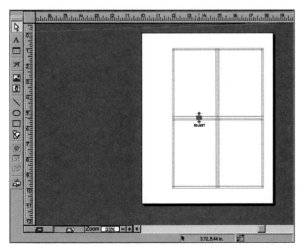

End

How to Use Ruler Guides

Sometimes you have specific pages filled with elements that should be aligned in an attractive and professional manner. Aligning those elements is easy if you employ ruler guides on each page that needs this attention. A ruler guide lines up with a specific position on a ruler, and you can use it to determine the placement of frames.

These guides are created with the help of the rulers that appear on your **Publisher** window.

Begin

1 Select a Ruler

Select a ruler by holding down the **Shift** key as you position your pointer over a ruler. Your pointer turns into an **Adjust** pointer. If you need a vertical guide, use the ruler on the left side of the **Publisher** window. For a horizontal guide, use the ruler at the top of the **document** window.

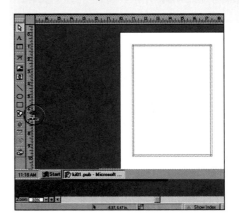

2 Drag the Ruler Guide

Drag your pointer to the appropriate position on the page. A **green line** indicates a ruler guide. (Don't worry, it doesn't print.)

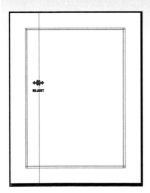

3 Adjust the Ruler Guide

You can adjust the positioning of any ruler guide by holding down the **Shift** key and positioning your pointer over the **green line** until your pointer turns into the **Adjust** pointer. Drag the guide to a new position. When you release the **Shift** key and the mouse button, the ruler guide is in the new position (the original **green line** disappears).

4 Adding Ruler Guides Quickly

You can use menu commands if you don't want to drag a ruler guide from the ruler. Choose **Arrange**, **Ruler Guides** from the **menu bar**. Select **Add Horizontal Ruler Guide** or **Add Vertical Ruler Guide** from the **submenu**.

5 Position the Ruler Guide

The ruler guide is placed in the center of the page when you use the menu commands. Follow Step 3 to adjust the position.

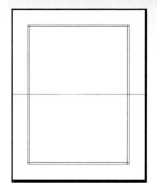

6 Deleting a Ruler Guide

To delete a single ruler guide, hold down the **Shift** key and position your mouse pointer over the guide until you see an **Adjust** pointer, and then drag the guide back to its ruler.

7 Deleting All Ruler Guides

If you want to remove all the ruler guides you've placed on a page, choose **Arrange**, **Ruler Guides**, **Clear All Ruler Guides** from the **menu bar**.

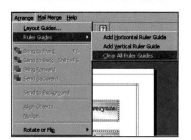

End

How to Change the View

You can change the way your **Publisher** window looks, or the way your publication appears in the window. This can make it easier to work, and can even make your work faster.

Begin

1 Hiding and Showing Guides

Having the guide lines visible makes it easy to position elements correctly. If you want to view your publication without the distractions of those colored lines, you can eliminate them from the **Publisher** window. Choose **View, Hide Boundaries and Guides** from the **menu bar**. To use the guides again, choose **View.** You'll see that the command has changed to **Show Boundaries and Guides**.

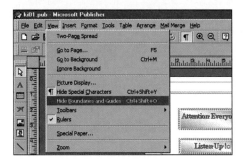

2 Viewing the Actual Size

You can view the page and its elements in actual size. (By default, Publisher uses a full-page view so you can see the entire page you're working on. However, you can use the zoom buttons on the **status bar** to move closer and farther away when you're working on a specific frame.) To see the actual size, right-click the **status bar** and choose **Actual Size** from the **shortcut menu** that pops up. To return to the default view, choose **Full Page** from the menu.

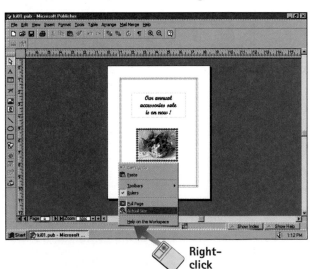

Right-click

3 Grabbing a Ruler

Whenever you're working with page elements that must be a specific size, you can note the size by looking at the rulers in the **Publisher** window. However, it's more accurate (and easier on the eyes) to bring the ruler to the element. To do this, position your pointer over the ruler until the pointer becomes a **double-headed arrow**. Drag the ruler to the frame you want to measure.

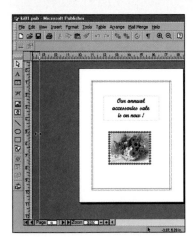

4 Using the Ruler to Resize

The ruler appears when you release the mouse. You can move or resize the frame to match the measurements you need. For information on moving and resizing frames, see Chapter 2's Task 2, "How to Move and Resize Text Frames," and Chapter 3's Tasks 3 "How to Move, Resize, and Crop Shapes," and 17, "How to Move, Resize, and Crop Graphic Frames." (Drag the ruler back to its original spot when you've finished using it.)

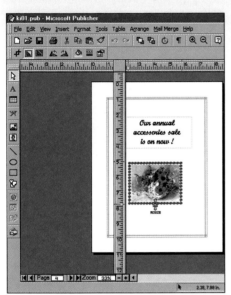

5 Changing the Display of Pictures

If you have complicated, busy pictures (graphic images with a lot of elements and details), moving through your document can become a slow process. That's because Publisher has to draw the picture(s) on the page as you move to each page. To change the way pictures display, choose **View**, **Picture Display** from the **menu bar**.

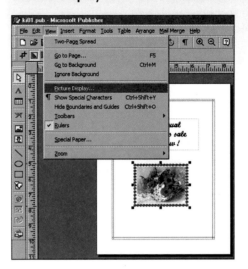

6 Choosing a Picture Display Mode

When the **Picture Display** dialog box opens, select a new display mode. You might want to try both alternatives to see which one works best for you. Choose **OK** to save your selection.

How-To Hints

Viewing and Hiding Toolbars

Just like most Windows software, Publisher has choices on the **View** menu for viewing and hiding toolbars and the ruler. If you don't need one or more of these elements (at least for the moment), getting rid of them gives you more room to work in the **document** window.

End

How to Use Publisher Help

One very noticeable difference between Publisher 98 and all the other Windows software you use is the way the **Help** files work. You can access them from the **menu** (**Help**, **Contents**, or **Help**, **Index**), but it's faster to use the **Show Index** and **Show Help** buttons on the right side of the **status bar**.

Begin

1 Open the Help Files

Click **Show Index** to open the **Help** index (the **Help Contents** page also opens). Click **Show Help** to open the **Help Contents** window.

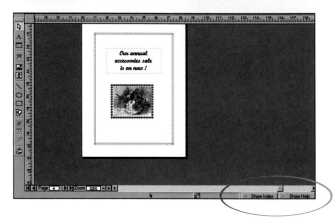

2 Using the Index

The most efficient way to find help on a subject is to use the index. Enter a word that reflects the subject you need help on; the **Index** window moves to the section of the index that contains that subject.

3 Pick the Topic

Select the topic or a subtopic (if there are subtopics listed) to see the associated **Help** page in the right pane (the **contents** pane).

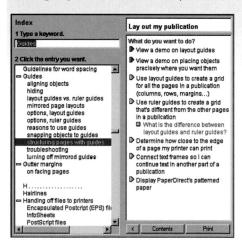

4 Using a Help Page with Lists

There are a variety of **Help** page types in Publisher. If the **Help** page offers a list of topics, place your pointer on the **arrow** next to the listing you want to investigate (your pointer turns into a **hand**). Click to open that Help topic, which is frequently another list that narrows the topic. Find the topic of interest and click its **arrow**.

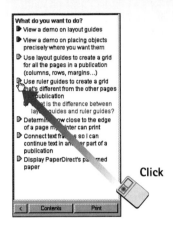

Click

5 Getting More Information

Many **Help** pages have a tab named **More Info**. After you've read the **Help** page (and followed any step-by-step instructions), click the **More Info** tab.

6 Choose a Demo

Click the listing of interest in the **More Info** tab. Many of the **More Info** tabs have a listing for a demo, in addition to other subjects related to your original query. Click the **arrow** next to the demo listing.

Click

7 Viewing a Demo

Use the **arrows** in the **demo** window to move through the demo. (The first **arrow** returns you to the first page. You can also click the **Print** button to print the demo pages. Click **Done** to close the **demo** window.)

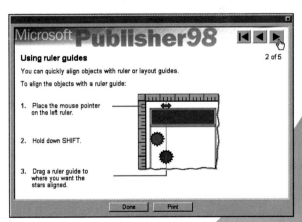

Continues

How to Use Publisher Help Continued

You can read explanatory information in the **Help** pages, follow the steps to complete a task, or view a demo—but that's not all. There are more features available.

8 Using Topic Overview Windows

Some index selections produce a box that contains information about the subject you selected. This is how Publisher offers explanations and overviews of major subjects. Scroll through the **topic** window to learn about the subject or use the **Print** button to print it. Click **Done** to close the **topic** window.

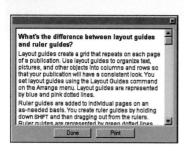

9 Ask a Troubleshooting Question

Many of the topics have a listing named **Troubleshoot** in the index pane. Click it to see the **Troubleshoot** window for that topic, and then choose the listing that best describes your problem.

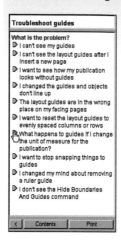

10 Read the Troubleshooting Suggestions

Troubleshoot windows can have explanations, suggestions, steps to follow, additional listings, or any combination of these things. You can use the **Print** button to get a hard copy of the window's contents. Choose **Done** to close the **Troubleshoot** window.

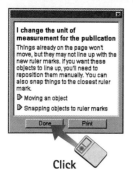

Click

11 Go Back

The **contents** pane has a less-than sign (<), which works as a "go-back-one-pane" feature. Click it to move to the pane you viewed previously.

12 View All Contents

Click the **Contents** button at the bottom of the **contents** pane to see an overview of the features available in Publisher and what you can accomplish with those tools. (This is the closest the Help system comes to the **contents** pane of most Windows software **Help** files.)

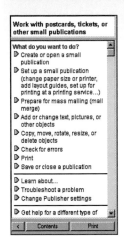

13 Get Definitions

Contents that are blue are definitions (although many of them go beyond simple definitions and have rather full explanations). Click to see the information.

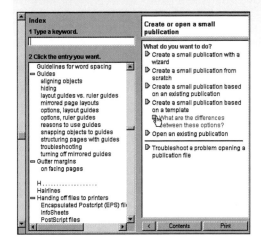

14 Close the Help Windows

To close the **Index** window, choose **Hide Index**. (You can continue navigating through the **Help Contents** window.) To close both **Help** windows, choose **Hide Help**.

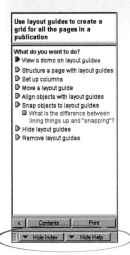

End

How to Get Help from Microsoft

Microsoft maintains a Web site for Publisher, and you can go there without closing the software.

If your browser doesn't automatically connect to your Internet service provider when you launch it, you have to establish the connection before you use the steps discussed here.

Begin

1 Choose the Command

Choose **Help, Microsoft Publisher Web Site** from the **menu bar**. This command launches your browser and points it to the Publisher Web site.

2 Register Publisher

The Publisher site is replete with help, information, and other features. You should start by selecting **REGISTRATION** from the **navigator bar** (unless you've already taken care of that). After you register your copy of Publisher, you can take advantage of all of Microsoft's support.

3 Get Support

Click **SUPPORT** on the **navigator bar** to get help on Publisher.

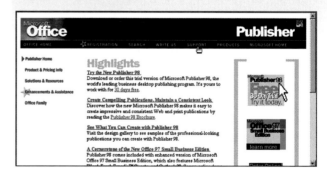

4 Choose Publisher and Select a Search Method

In the **Support Online** window, click the **arrow** to the right of step **1** and select **Publisher** from the list that displays; then select the search option you want to use in step **2**.

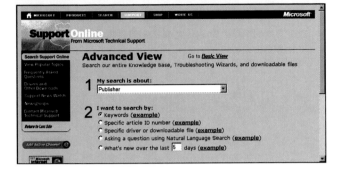

5 Enter a Query

The page jumps to step **3**. Type a word or short phrase that is related to the Help topic you're looking for. The text that Microsoft placed in the box is deleted as soon as you start typing your own text. The default options for searching work best, so don't bother to change them. Click **find** to begin your search.

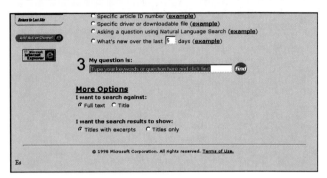

6 Scan the Articles

A list of articles related to your query is displayed in the window, along with a reminder of the word(s) you entered. The first couple of lines from each article are displayed to give you an idea of the contents. Click any article that seems to provide the help you need.

7 Using the Article

If a helpful article is available, use the tools on your browser to select it and then you can copy it to a word processor (or Notepad). You can also print it. Use the **navigation** buttons on your browser to return to the list of articles. Continue until you have found all the available information on the topic.

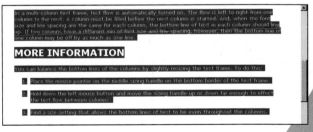

Continues

How to Get Help from Microsoft Continued

In addition to technical support, there are lots of other features on the Publisher Web site you can take advantage of.

8 Enhancements and Tips

Click the link to **Enhancements & Assistance**. Microsoft updates the Web site frequently, so you may not see the exact listing shown here. However, there's always a listing that refers to enhancements.

9 Examine the New Features

Select the link to **Publisher Enhancements**.

Get the Most Out of Publisher with Office Update

Back to Publisher

If you own Publisher 97 or any Office 97 application, you can take advantage of Office Update, an online resource containing a wealth of articles, tips, add-ins, and more -- all created to help you get the most out of Office 97.

☆ Publisher Enhancements
Download additional templates, add-ins, and more.

☆ Publisher Assistance
Check out the latest timesaving tips and advice.

Want to Know More About Office Update?
You can learn more about Office Update before signing up. Or you can join now.

© 1998 Microsoft Corporation
All rights reserved. Terms of use.

10 Find a File to Download

Scroll through the list (there's usually more than one page of lists), and if you find something of interest, follow the instructions to download it.

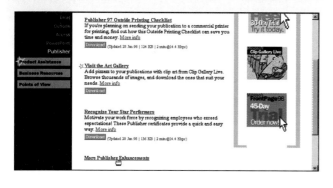

11 Find Tips and Tricks

Use your browser's **Back** button to return to the page that displayed the links. Look for a link to tips and tricks and select it. (The title for this link may change from time to time, but there's always a link for tips.)

Get the Most Out of Publisher with Office Update

Back to Publisher

If you own Publisher 97 or any Office 97 application, you can take advantage of Office Update, an online resource containing a wealth of articles, tips, add-ins, and more -- all created to help you get the most out of Office 97.

☆ Publisher Enhancements
Download additional templates, add-ins, and more.

☆ Publisher Assistance
Check out the latest timesaving tips and advice.

Want to Know More About Office Update?
You can learn more about Office Update before signing up. Or you can join now.

12 Select an Article

Scroll through the articles and find the ones you want. Click each listing to jump to the article, and then use the tools on your browser to copy or print it.

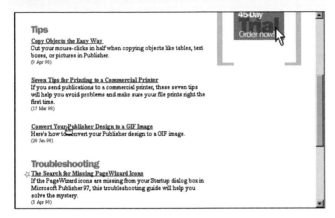

13 Using Search

Each Web page you visit has a **SEARCH** button available on the **navigation bar**. You can click it to avoid wandering through all the pages on the Publisher site in search of specific information.

14 Use the Search Engine Tools

Enter a word, a phrase, or a sentence in the **Search** text box. Make sure Publisher is selected in the **product** box, and then click the **Search** button to find all the information on the site that relates to your query.

End

How to Use the Office Assistant

I haven't met anyone with a mild reaction to the Office Assistant—people either love it or hate it. This animated character appeared first in Office 97 and then migrated to Publisher 98. It's available whenever you want a hint about your current task or if you have a specific question.

Begin

1 Call the Assistant

The Office Assistant is so eager to help that there is a wide choice of ways to call upon it: Press **F1**, choose **Help**, **Microsoft Publisher Help**, or click the **question mark** on the **Standard** toolbar.

2 Enter a Question

The Office Assistant shows up with a **yellow balloon**, ready for you to enter a question. As soon as you begin typing, the Office Assistant's message is deleted in order to make room for your characters.

3 Start the Search

Click **Search** to have the Office Assistant search the **Help** files for **Help** pages that contain your query.

4 Choose a Help Topic

Most of the time the Office Assistant offers a choice of Help topics that are related to your query. Select the one that seems to be on target. Click the **See more** arrow to see the additional topics that don't fit on the balloon.

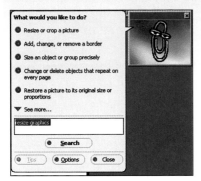

5 Read the Help Page

The **Help Contents** window opens so you can see the Help topic. If the Office Assistant is in the way, place your mouse pointer on the **blue bar** at the top of the box and drag it away. You can also click the **X** in the upper-right corner to close the box.

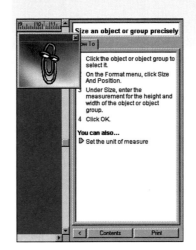

6 Change Your Query

If the list that appears seems too wide-ranging, you can change your query. Your original query is highlighted at the bottom of the **balloon**—just type your new phrase to replace the highlighted text automatically.

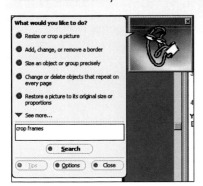

Continues

How to Use the Office Assistant Continued

The Office Assistant doesn't just answer questions, it can also guess what you need to know.

In addition, you can configure the Office Assistant's behavior, and you can even change the persona.

7 Call the Assistant for Specific Help

If you perform a task (creating a picture frame on a page, for example), the Office Assistant is prepared with specific Help recommendations when you call it. (Your last query also appears in the balloon, and you can replace it with a new query if the listing in the balloon isn't what you need.)

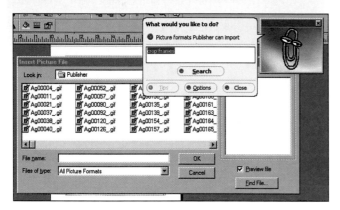

8 Closing the Balloon

Some people prefer to leave the Office Assistant on the desktop all the time. Clicking the **Close** button on the balloon leaves the Assistant on the desktop. To open a balloon so you can enter a query, click the **bar** on the top of the Assistant's box.

9 Configure the Office Assistant

Click the balloon's **Options** button to configure the behavior of the Office Assistant.

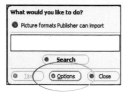

10 Setting Options

Select the options you want from the **Options** tab of the **Office Assistant** dialog box.

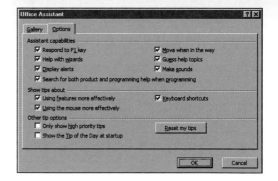

11 Change the Office Assistant Persona

You can select a different Office Assistant (perhaps you have a problem with paper clips). Click the **Gallery** tab in the **Office Assistant** dialog box.

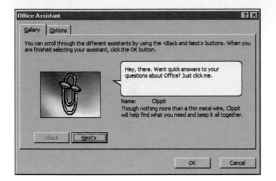

12 Move Through the Gallery

Click **Next** to move through the Office Assistant characters available to you and choose the one you like best; then click **OK**.

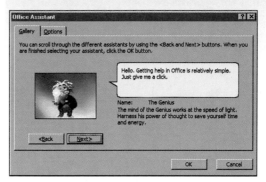

End

How-To Hints

The Assistant Has Sound Effects

If you have a sound card, that metallic noise you hear is from the Office Assistant. It's supposed to be the sound of a paper clip.

How to Save and Retrieve Publications

Saving and retrieving documents are necessary processes, no matter what software you're using.

Begin

1 Choose a Save Command

You have several choices for issuing the Save command: Click the **Save** button on the **Standard toolbar**; press **Ctrl+S**; or choose **File, Save** from the **menu bar**. The first two options are easier and faster than the **menu bar** option.

2 Saving for the First Time

The first time you save a publication, the **Save As** dialog box appears so you can enter a name for the file. Click **Save** after entering that name. As you continue to work, you can use any of the methods enumerated in Step 1 to continue to save your work.

3 Publisher Reminders

Publisher automatically reminds you to save every 15 minutes. This nagging message is really a form of insurance for you.

4 Retrieving a File from the Catalog

When you first open Publisher (which opens the Catalog), move to the Catalog's **Existing Publications** tab. The last four files you worked on are listed in the top section of the left pane, and a complete list of your saved publications is displayed below that. Click a filename to see a preview of the first page in the right pane as a reminder of the file's contents. Double-click the file you want to open.

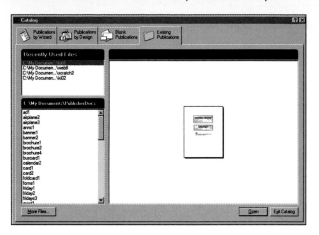

5 Opening a File

If you're working in Publisher, you can use the standard Windows functions for opening a file. Click the **Open** button on the **Standard** toolbar (or, if you prefer the long way, choose **File**, **Open** from the **menu bar**). When the **Open** dialog box appears, select the file you want to work on.

6 Closing a File

Choose **File**, **Close** to close a file so you can work on another file. (Publisher permits only one file at a time, unlike other Windows software.) If you've made changes since the last time you saved the file, you're given an opportunity to save the file before it's closed.

7 Saving with a Different Name

If you want to save a file under a different filename, choose **File**, **Save As** from the **menu bar**. This is useful for making a copy of a file in which you've made changes, but you're not sure if you like the changes. Now you have a copy of the file with and without your experimental elements.

End

How to Set Options for Publisher

As you use and become comfortable with Publisher, you should change its behavior to match the way you want to work. There are plenty of customization options available to accomplish this.

Begin

1 Changing Options

Choose **Tools**, **Options** from the **menu bar**.

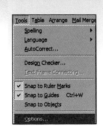

2 Setting General Options

When the **Options** dialog box appears, the **General** tab is in the foreground. There are quite a few important customizations you can effect in this tab.

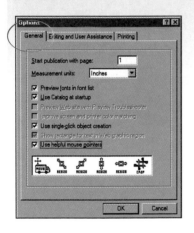

3 Change the Font List

By default, Publisher shows you the font list with each font displaying its appearance. If you find this annoying, click the **Preview fonts in font list** option on the **General** tab to remove the check mark. Now your font list appears in plain type (which you may find much easier to read).

4 Start with a Blank Page

After you've been using Publisher for a while, you may prefer to start every publication from scratch. To open Publisher and see a blank page, click the **Use Catalog at startup** option to remove the check mark. (If you occasionally need the Catalog, just choose **File**, **New** from the **menu bar**.)

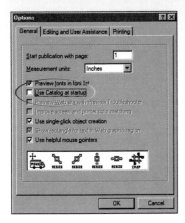

5 Creating Frames with a Click

If you click the box next to the **Use single-click object creation** option to deselect it, frames won't pop into your publication with a mouse click. Instead, you must drag each frame to create it (which means you size it to your specifications as you create it). Some people find this easier because they accidentally click and then have to resize the frame.

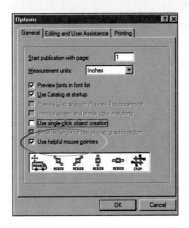

6 Pointers with Messages

When you are dragging, sizing, moving, or otherwise manipulating frames, your mouse pointer displays a different shape and also displays text to indicate its current status. If you deselect this option, the pointers change to a different shape and there's no text reminder. You can deselect the **Use helpful mouse pointers** option if you prefer.

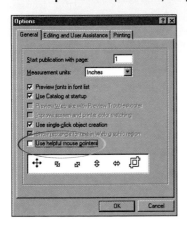

7 Other General Options

There are two options that aren't commonly changed at the top of the **General** tab, but you may find either (or both) necessary for the way you work. You can specify a new number in the **Start publication with page** box if you don't want your first page number to be 1. This is useful if the publications you create are inserted in predesigned covers that use Page 1 (and Page 2 if printed on both sides). Change the **Measurement units** to **Centimeters**, **Picas**, or **Points** if you don't want to work with inches.

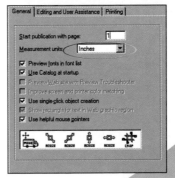

Continues

8 Setting Other Options

Move to the **Editing and User Assistance** tab in the **Options** dialog box to select and deselect the configuration options. Start with the dialog box's **Text editing** section, where the options are self explanatory (and are the same as word-processing software options).

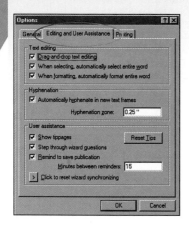

9 Set Hyphenation

You can turn off automatic hyphenation or change the hyphenation zone to alter the way automatic hyphenation works. The *zone* is the amount of space between the last character on a line and the right margin. Making the zone smaller increases the number of hyphens (and vice versa). For more information about hyphenation, read Chapter 5's Task 4, "How to Perfect Hyphenation."

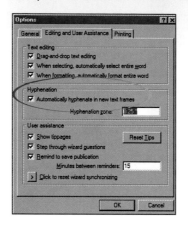

10 Set Assistance Options

The dialog box's **User assistance** section has options you can change to increase or decrease the amount of unasked-for help that Publisher provides.

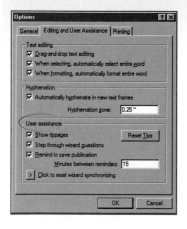

11 Reset Synchronization

Click the button named **Click to reset wizard synchronizing** to reset the current document's synchronization (this option isn't a global option). *Synchronization* is a Publisher feature that coordinates special data such as personal information to make sure everything in the document agrees. See the next section, "How to Use Personal Information Sets," for more details about this special data.

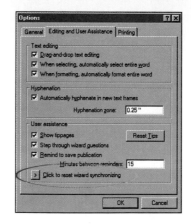

12 Configure Printing for Publications

Move to the **Printing** tab in the **Options** dialog box to set the global options for printing (which are self explanatory).

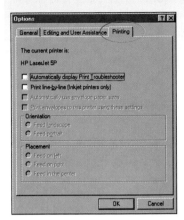

13 Configure Printing for Envelopes

If the current document is an envelope, more choices become available in the **Options** dialog box's **Printing** tab. Select **Print envelopes to this printer using these settings**, and then specify the way you handle envelopes for the printer.

Click

14 Save Your New Options

When you have finished selecting and deselecting options on all the tabs, click **OK** to save your settings.

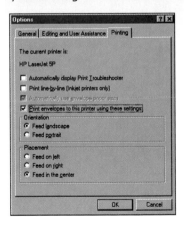

End

How-To Hints

First Time User Assistance

Using some Publisher features for the first time (for instance, typing in the overflow section of a text frame) produces a yellow information message. Subsequent use of the same feature doesn't bring up that information, but if you want to see them again you can click the **Reset Tips** button. (See Step 10.)

How to Use Personal Information Sets

Because so many people use Publisher to design stationery and other personalized publications, Publisher provides a way to save the information that appears (your name, address, and so on). These personal information sets provide a way to enter the information once and then insert it in all your publications, instead of typing it each time you create a publication.

There are four personal information sets (PISs): Primary Business, Secondary Business, Other Organization, and Home/Family.

The Primary Business PIS is attached to each publication by default. Publisher inserts some data into that PIS automatically by using the information you provided when you installed Publisher.

Begin

1 Select a PIS

To attach a PIS to a publication and use its data, choose **Insert**, **Personal Information**, **Select**; choose a PIS from the **submenu**. (The **Primary Business PIS** is selected by default.)

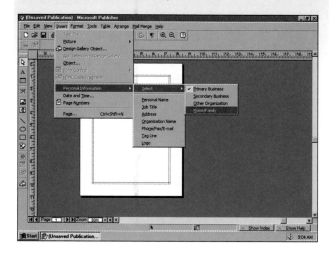

2 Insert Data

If you selected any PIS except Primary Business, you can also create the data for the new PIS as you enter data. Choose **Insert**, **Personal Information**, and then select the data item you want to insert in your publication.

3 Check the Data

A text box appears in the center of your **Publisher** window—it contains the data you inserted. Press **F9** to zoom in to read it and change it if you prefer. Publisher copies the information from the Primary Business PIS into each PIS, so you'll often find you have to change the data when you're working with a different PIS—although you probably won't have to change your name.

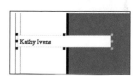

4 Position the Data

Press **F9** to zoom out and then move the text frame to the appropriate position on the page. Read Chapter 2's Task 2, "How to Move and Resize Text Frames," to learn about moving text frames. Continue to add and change data; position it on your page. When you save the publication, you save the PIS data you selected. The next time you select that PIS for a publication, the data you edited is inserted.

5 Colorizing a PIS

You can colorize the information that's inserted from a PIS. Open a publication that has the PIS you want to use. Choose **Format, Color Scheme** from the **menu bar**. When the **Color Scheme** dialog box opens, make your changes; then select the **Include scheme in Personal Information** check box.

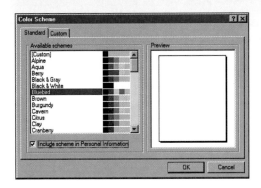

6 Make the Change Permanent

A message appears, telling you that if you include the PIS in the color-scheme formatting, all publications connected to this PIS will use this color scheme. Most of the time this is just dandy, because as you create stationery and other publications for an entity represented by a PIS, you want the color schemes to be the same. Of course, you can always change the schemes for any individual publication. Depending on your feelings, choose **OK** or **Cancel**.

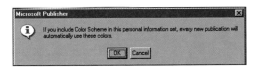

End

How-To Hints

Quick Tip for Creating Data

Here's how to enter all the data you need for each PIS: Open a blank document, select a PIS (start with Primary Business), and insert each available component. After you enter the data for all the components, save the publication with a filename like **bizpisdata**. Repeat for each PIS (using filenames such as **familypisdata**). If you ever have to change any PIS data, just open the appropriate publication and make the changes. When you save the publication, you also save the new data in the PIS; it will be changed in every publication that uses that PIS.

Task

2

Working with Text

You'll probably devote a great deal of space to text in most of your publications. You have a message, a story, an article—you have something to say—and that's frequently the most important part of your publication. In fact, if all you needed to do was show a bunch of images, you'd probably be using different software (like Microsoft PowerPoint, which is designed to make slide shows instead of publications).

The text you present in your publication will have more impact if it's professionally presented. That means you must pay attention to the size of text as well as the way it lays out. Headlines have a purpose, as do body text and lists. Laying out your document so that each text element has the right effect on the reader is part of learning to create slick publications.

Whether you're making an announcement with a headline, drawing attention to a picture, or telling a story that crosses several pages, Publisher has tools to assist you. In this chapter you learn how to use those tools. ●

How to Create a Text Frame

The one thing all your publications will have in common is text. You have something to say, to report, or to sell, and that takes words.

You can't just start typing on a Publisher page; you have to start with a text frame.

Begin

1 Click Text Frame Tool

Click the **Text Frame** tool on the **Objects** toolbar.

Click

2 Starting a Text Frame

Place your pointer at the location where you want the upper-left corner of your text frame to be. Your pointer has changed to a crosshair.

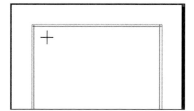

3 Drag Out a Frame

Hold down the left mouse button as you drag down and to the right to form the text frame.

Release the mouse button when the frame is the proper size and shape.

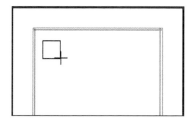

4 Creating a Vertical Rectangle

If you want a vertical rectangle (or you're not comfortable dragging the mouse), click the **Text Frame** tool and position your mouse where you want the center of the text frame to be.

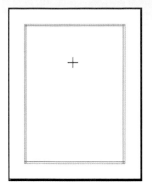

5 Just Click

Click once to place a text frame on your publication page.

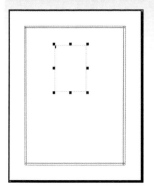

6 Undoing Mistakes

If you don't like the text frame or its position on the page, click the **Undo** button on the **Standard** toolbar. Then start again.

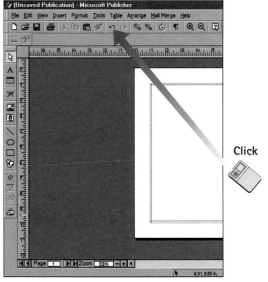

Click

End

How-To Hints

Add Frames to the Wizard's Design

If you used a wizard to design your publication, there are already text frames in place. However, many times you'll want to insert additional text frames to hold special information such as headings. You'll probably have to make room for a new frame by changing the size of existing frames. See "How to Move and Resize Text Frames" on the next page.

How to Resize and Move Text Frames

There are a slew of reasons that make it necessary to resize or move text frames. If you use the one-click method of creating text frames, you almost always have to change the size—Publisher can't read your mind. Sometimes you have too much text and have to make the frame larger (or too little text and you want a smaller frame). Then there are all those times you have to decide whether a heading should appear above or below an illustration, so you move the frame up and down until you like what you see.

Begin

1 Select a Frame

Click the frame to select it, which causes sizing handles to appear around the frame.

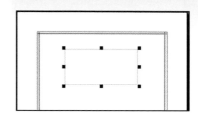

2 Moving Any Side of a Frame

To move any side of a frame, either to make it larger or smaller, place your pointer on one of the sizing handles along the side. Your pointer turns into a **Resize** pointer.

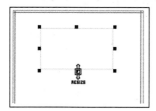

3 Drag to Resize a Frame

Press and hold down the left mouse button as you drag the sizing handle in the appropriate direction. Release the mouse button when the side is where you want it.

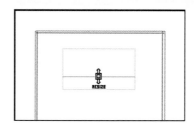

4 Resizing Multiple Sides Simultaneously

To change two sides at the same time, place your mouse pointer on one of the corner sizing handles. Your pointer turns into a **Resize** pointer again, but this time it's on an angle. Drag the corner and watch both sides come along.

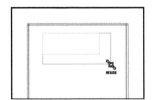

5 Change Opposite Sides Equally

To keep the center of the text frame centered (which means an equal movement on the opposite side), hold down the **Ctrl** key while you drag.

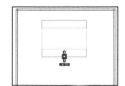

6 Move the Frame

To move a text frame, place your pointer on the outside edge of the frame between any two sizing handles. Your pointer turns into a moving van. Press and hold the left mouse button as you move the text frame to a new location.

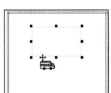

End

How-To Hints

Cancel Your Dragging Action

If you change your mind while you're dragging, press the **Esc** key to cancel the drag.

How to Enter Text and Use the Text Formatting Toolbar

Of course, the important ingredient in a text frame is the message. After your text frame is positioned on your page, it's time to start entering the words you need in order to get your message to the reader.

As you're entering text, don't worry about the word wrap or the positioning—you can adjust the text and the frame later.

Begin

1 Locating the Insertion Point

When you create a text frame, your insertion point waits for your data entry in the upper-left corner of the frame. You must select the text frame (click anywhere in the frame) to see the insertion point.

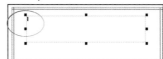

2 Highlight Placeholder

If you're working on a predesigned publication, click anywhere in the text frame to highlight the existing placeholder text. As soon as you type the first character of your own text, the placeholder text is deleted.

3 Can't See What You're Typing?

By default your publication is zoomed out so you can see the layout. This makes it impossible to see what you're typing.

4 Zoom In

Press **F9** to zoom in. Enter your text, which is much easier now that you can see what you're doing.

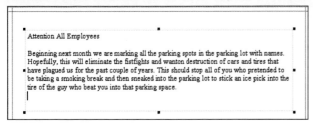

5 Zoom Back Out

Press **F9** again to zoom out, so you can see the results in your layout. Click anywhere outside the text frame to deselect it, which gives you a better view of the layout.

6 Text Formatting Toolbar Appears

When you select a text frame, the **Text Formatting** toolbar appears below the **Standard** toolbar in your **Publisher** window. In the next few pages you use the tools available on the toolbar, so this is a good time to go over them.

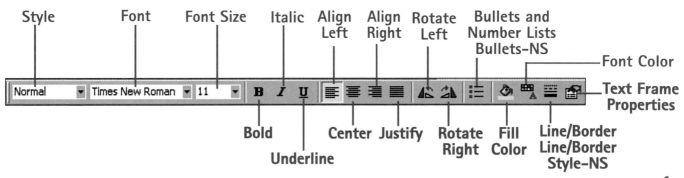

End

How-To Hints

No Double Spaces

Professional publications have only one space after the punctuation at the end of a sentence.

Use the Clipboard

If you created your text in a word processor, you can use the Windows Clipboard to copy and paste between the two software applications.

How to Format Text Appearance

There's nothing more boring (and unprofessional) than plain, unformatted text. Blah! No matter what your message is (even if it's on a boring topic), it's more effective to use special formatting to add pizzazz.

Notice that as soon as you click anywhere in a text frame, the frame is selected and the **Text Formatting** toolbar appears in your **Publisher** window.

Begin

1 Select Text

Select the text you want to format. You can drag your mouse across the text to select it, or use the keyboard shortcuts listed in the How-To Hints on the next page.

Attention All Employees

Beginning next month we are marking all the parking spots in the parking lot with names. Hopefully, this will eliminate the fistfights and wanton destruction of cars and tires that have plagued us for the past couple of years. This should stop all of you who pretended to be taking a smoking break and then sneaked into the parking lot to stick an ice pick into the tire of the guy who beat you into that parking space.

2 Formatting Text

Click the appropriate icon on the **Text Formatting** toolbar. For example, you may want to make the text bold. The text accepts the formatting change and remains highlighted so you can continue to format it.

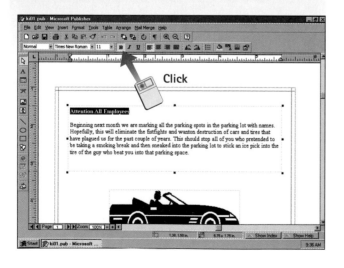

Click

3 Changing Fonts

To change the font, click the arrow to the right of the font box and choose a new font. As a shortcut, you can begin entering the characters of the font name to move to that section of the font list quickly. (To change the font size, click the arrow to the right of the **font size** box and select a new size.)

Click

4 Additional Format Choices

To see more formatting choices than the toolbar provides, choose **Format**, **Font** from the **menu bar**. Then specify the formatting you want in the **Font** dialog box.

5 Adjust Spacing Between Letters

You can adjust the spacing between letters in the **Character Spacing** dialog box, which you open by choosing **Format**, **Character Spacing** from the **menu bar**.

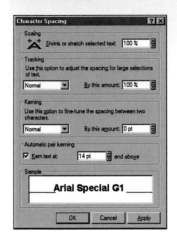

6 Adjust Spacing Between Lines

Change the spacing between lines with the **Line Spacing** dialog box. This is very effective if you have lists. Choose **Format**, **Line Spacing** from the **menu bar**.

7 Problems with Text Fitting

Some formatting changes enlarge the text and the space it occupies. If the text no longer fits within the text frame, Publisher flashes a warning message. Don't worry, you haven't lost any text, even if you can't see it all. You can learn how to work with this situation in Chapter 2, Task 8's "How to Work with Overflow Text."

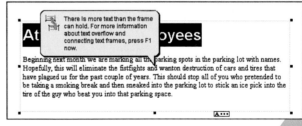

End

How to Create Special Text Effects

In addition to the common formatting changes that alter the appearance of characters, you may need to create some special effects for your text. These effects are frequently employed as attention-getting techniques.

Begin

1 Select Text

Select the text you want to format.

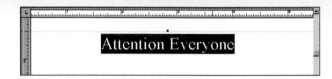

2 Colorizing Text

To colorize the text, click the **Font Color** icon on the **Text Formatting** toolbar. The colors that fit into your selected color scheme are displayed, and you can click the color you want for this text.

3 Additional Text Colors

Choose **More Colors** to see a larger palette, and then select the color you want to use. Choose **OK** to return to your page, where your text is still highlighted (so you can't see the color). Click anywhere outside the text frame to see the effect.

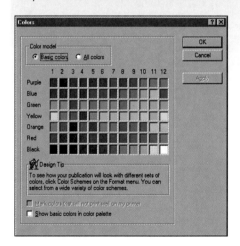

4 Rotating Text 90 Degrees

To rotate the text frame 90 degrees, click the frame to select it and click the **Rotate Left** or **Rotate Right** icon on the **Text Formatting** toolbar.

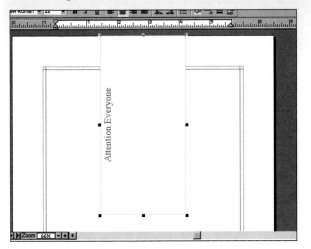

5 Rotating Text Other than 90 Degrees

To rotate the frame by a different number of degrees, select the frame and click the **Custom Rotate** icon on the **Standard** toolbar. In the **Custom Rotate** dialog box, specify the degrees and direction. Rotating text frames usually requires a further step of resizing, moving, or both.

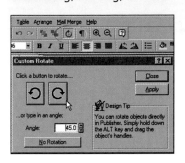

6 Adding Drop Caps

To add a drop cap, select the frame and choose **Format**, **Drop Cap** from the **menu bar** to open the **Drop Cap** dialog box. Choose a drop-cap style and see the effect in the Preview frame.

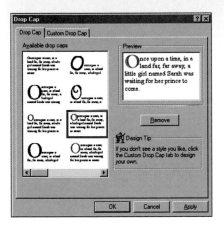

7 Customizing Drop Caps

To design your own drop cap, move to the **Custom Drop Cap** tab and select the settings you want. Choose **Apply** to see the effect, and then tweak until it's perfect. Choose **OK** to save the drop cap.

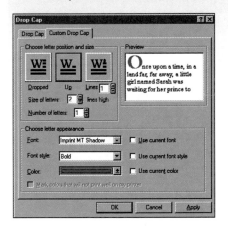

End

How to Create Lists

Sometimes important information stands out more effectively if you create a list. Because there's nothing more boring than a list of sentences on a page, Publisher provides ways to make your lists more interesting. Even better, Publisher automates the work involved so you really don't have much to do (except tweak the formatting to make it suit your own taste).

You can create bullet lists or numbered lists with equal ease. Of course, you must create a text frame before using lists.

If you've already entered a list and want to change it to a bullet or numbered list, select the text and then use the tools described here to convert the text to lists.

Begin

1 Beginning a List

To begin entering a list, position your pointer where the list starts and click the **Bullets** icon on the **Text Formatting** toolbar.

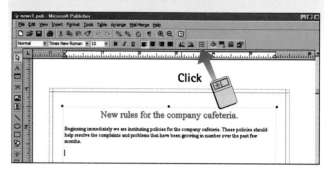

Click

2 Select a Bullet Type

For a bullet list, select one of the bullet characters displayed on the drop-down menu.

3 Enter Text

The bullet character appears in your text frame. Enter your text, which is automatically indented from the bullet character. When you press **Enter**, the next bullet appears and you can enter the next list item.

Beginning immediately we are instituting policies for the company cafeteria. These policies should help resolve the complaints and problems that have been growing in number over the past few months.

◆ Names must be clearly marked on any containers placed in the refrigerator.
◆

4 Creating a Numbered List

For a numbered list, choose **More Bullets** from the **drop-down menu** shown in Step 2. In the **Indents and Lists** dialog box, select the **Numbered List** option.

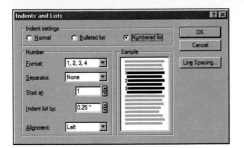

5 Ending a List

When you want to end the list and resume normal text, click the **Bullets** icon on the **Text Formatting** toolbar and choose **None**.

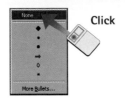

Click

6 Changing Bullet Appearance

You can tweak the formatting for bullets in the **Indents and Lists** dialog box. Bullet size, indentation, and alignment can be altered. Choose **Line Spacing** to see the **Line Spacing** dialog box, where you can make further changes to the appearance of the bullet list.

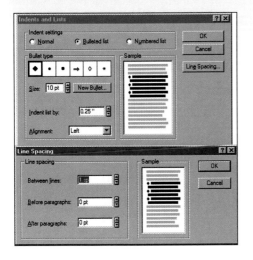

7 Changing Numbered List Appearance

Select the **Numbered List** option in the **Indents and List** dialog box to tweak the formatting for numbered lists. You can change the **Format** to letters instead of numbers, specify **Line Spacing**, and insert a **Separator** (such as a period, comma, bracket, colon, and the like) after the number.

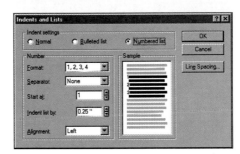

End

How-To Hints

Change the Start Number

If you interrupt a numbered list with regular text and want to pick up the numbering where you left off, use the **Start At** field in the **Indents and Lists** dialog box to specify the new starting number.

How to Create Columns in Text Frames

If you need columns in a text frame, you can create them manually, without changing your whole publication to a column format.

By default, all columns are the same width and are separated by the same amount of spacing when you establish columns for a text frame. However, this exercise provides some tricks to override that default configuration.

Begin

1 Click Text Frame Properties Icon

Click the text frame to select it, and then click the **Text Frame Properties** icon on the **Text Formatting** toolbar.

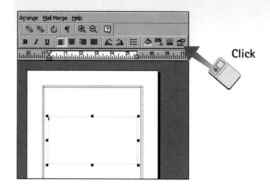

Click

2 Specify Number of Columns

In the **Text Frame Properties** dialog box, specify the **Number** of columns and the **Spacing** between them.

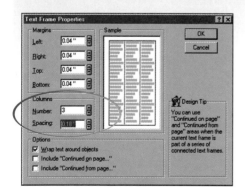

3 Entering Text

Begin entering text. As you reach the bottom of a column, the text wraps to the next column automatically.

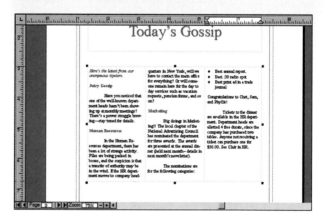

4 Resizing Frames

You can resize the text frame to tweak the appearance of the frame and the page.

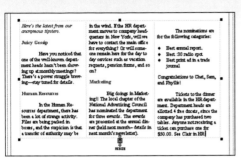

5 Creating Uneven Columns

To create uneven columns, create multiple text frames of different sizes.

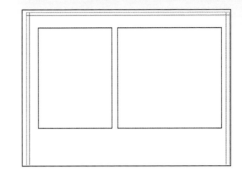

6 Using Text Frame Properties

Select one text frame and use the **Text Frame Properties** dialog box to create columns for that frame. (You can repeat the process for another frame if your design warrants it.)

How-To Hints

Forcing Text to Another Column

To force text to move to the top of the next column, press **Ctrl+Shift+Enter**.

End

How to Work with Overflow Text

When you have a great deal to say, there may be too much text to fit in your text frame. If there's a small amount of extra text, you can probably re-solve the problem with one of these easy methods:

- Edit the text to remove extraneous words. (Get rid of those multiple adverbs or use shorter adjectives.)
- Change to a smaller font size.
- Enlarge the text frame.

Frequently, however, you'll want to continue your story or article in a different frame (especially if you're designing a newsletter and want to continue a story on another page).

Begin

1 Entering Text into a Frame

As you're entering text, you're unable to see what you're typing when you reach the end of the text frame. The text isn't lost—it's just out of sight. The first time this happens, Publisher flashes a message. (Click it to make it go away.)

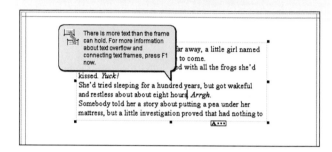

2 Inserting Text from Clipboard

If you insert text from the Clipboard (perhaps you copied it from your word processor), Publisher warns you if there's too much text. Choose **No** to refuse the offer to handle the problem auto-matically; you'll have far more control by using the manual steps you're learning here.

3 Text Overflow Indicator Button

To notify you that the overflow text exists, a **Text in Overflow indicator** button appears at the bottom of the text frame.

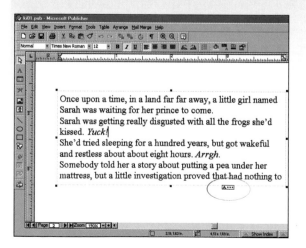

4 Connecting Text Frames

Create a text frame on the page in which you want to continue the story. Return to the original text frame and click it to select it. Choose **Tools**, **Text Frame Connecting** from the **menu bar**.

5 Connecting Text Frames

The **Connect Frames** toolbar appears. Click the **Connect Text Frames** icon. Your pointer turns into a **pitcher**. (The pitcher is holding all the text in the overflow area.)

Once upon a time, in a land far far away, a little girl named Sarah was waiting for her prince to come.
Sarah was getting really disgusted with all the frogs she'd kissed. *Yuck!*
She'd tried sleeping for a hundred years, but got waken and restless about about eight hours. *Arrgh.*
Somebody told her a story about putting a pea under her mattress, but a little investigation proved that had nothing to

Click

6 Pouring Text into a Frame

Move to the frame you created to hold the overflow text. When you position your mouse over the frame, the **pitcher** tilts. (It's getting ready to pour the text into the frame.)

7 Going to a Previous Frame

Click anywhere on the frame to pour the text into it. A **Go To Previous Frame** button is on the top of the frame, and you can click it to move to the frame that holds the beginning of your story (which now has a **Go To Next Frame** button). Click the **X** in the upper-right corner of the **Connect Frames** toolbar to close it.

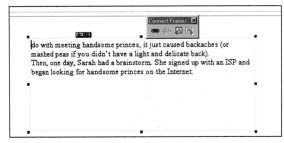

do with meeting handsome princes, it just caused backaches (or mashed peas if you didn't have a light and delicate back).
Then, one day, Sarah had a brainstorm. She signed up with an ISP and began looking for handsome princes on the Internet.

End

How to Create Continued Notices

If a story or an article is continued on a different page, you can add instructions for the reader. The phrases "Continued on page whatever" and "Continued from page whatever" let the reader move through your story smoothly. Publisher takes care of everything automatically, and even inserts the right page numbers.

Begin

1 Select a Frame

Click the first frame of the story to select it, and then click the **Text Frame Properties** icon on the **Text Formatting** toolbar.

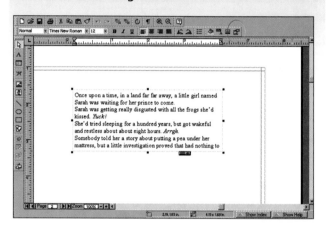

2 Select Continued on Page

In the **Text Frame Properties** dialog box, select **Include "Continued on page..."** and choose **OK**. Move to the text frame on which the article is continued and do the same thing, except select **Include "Continued from page..."**.

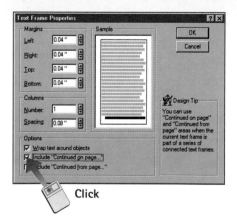

Click

3 Auto-Inserting a Page Number

Publisher automatically inserts the appropriate text and the page number.

urs. *Arrgh.*
putting a pea under her
(Continued on page 3)

4 Changing Wording of Notice

To change the wording of the notice, remove the text and enter your own phrase. Be careful not to remove the page number code.

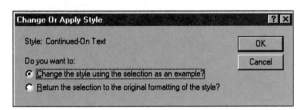

rgh.

; a pea under her

(Please turn to page 3)

5 Changing Formatting of Notice

To change the formatting of the notice, select it and use the formatting tools on the **Text Formatting** toolbar or the **menu bar** to change the appearance. In this case the font is changed.

> She'd tried sleeping for a hundred years, but got wakeful and restless about about eight hours. *Arrgh.*
> Somebody told her a story about putting a pea under her
>
> *(Please turn to page 3)*

6 Changing Style of Notice

To make the formatting changes permanent, you have to change the **Style** for the notice. Click anywhere in the text of the notice and then choose the style from the **Style** box. Select **Change the style** using the selection as an example and then choose **OK**. Repeat this process to change the **Continued From** notice.

7 Accidentally Deleting Page

If you accidentally delete the page number (which is really a code, not a number), you can replace the code. Position your pointer where you want the page number to appear in the notice and choose **Insert**, **Page Numbers** from the **menu bar**.

Click

End

How to Create a Style

If you have a bunch of formatting characteristics you want to apply to text, it's silly to reinvent the wheel each time you have to format. Instead, create a style that's composed of all those formatting commands and apply the style to any text that should be formatted with them.

Publisher 98 only provides a few preset styles for special types of text (such as the **Continued** notices discussed in the previous pages), so you have to create styles if you want them. Styles are created by example, which means you have to format text before you can create a style.

Begin

1 Select Word(s) to Format

Apply formatting characteristics to the appropriate text in order to create the example you need for a style. You only have to format a single word; you don't have to select the entire paragraph. (For instance, if you want to create a style for a section heading, select a heading and format one of the words within it.)

> **Juicy Gossip**
>
> Have you noticed that one of the well-known depart-

2 Click In the Style Box

Select the word you've formatted and click the **Style** box on the **Text Formatting** toolbar. As soon as you click, the default style (**Normal**, which is probably the only style) is highlighted.

3 Enter New Style Name

Enter the name for the new style (as soon as you begin typing, the highlighted text disappears and your new characters appear).

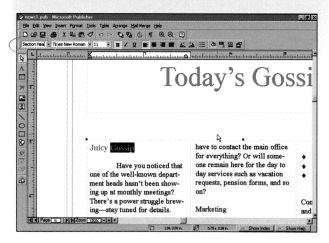

4 Saving New Style

Press **Enter**, which brings up the **Create Style By Example** dialog box. You can change the name of the style if you want to. Choose **OK** to save the style.

5 Applying the New Style

To use the style on other paragraphs that you want to format with the same characteristics, select the paragraph. Choose the style by clicking the **arrow** to the right of the **Style** box and selecting the style.

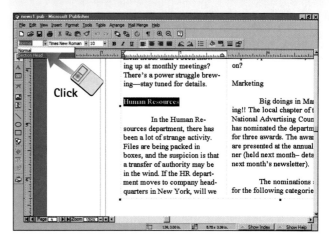

Click

6 Editing the New Style

To change the style, select any word that has been formatted with the style and make the formatting changes you need. Select the style from the **Style** box to bring up the **Change Or Apply Style** dialog box. Select **Change the style** using the selection as an example.

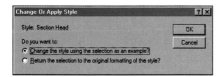

How-To Hints

You Can Import Your Styles

Styles you create are saved only in the current publication. If you want to use the style in other publications, you must import it. See the next task, "How to Import Styles from Publications," to learn how to import styles.

End

How to Import Styles from Publications

After you go to the trouble of creating styles in a publication, you can import those styles into other publications. This means, of course, that you aren't constantly reinventing the wheel. However, what is more important is the fact that having styles available in multiple publications gives your publications a consistency. That's an important concept as you strive to make your output as professional as possible.

Begin

1 Choose Text Style

Be sure the publication that needs the styles is the current document. Then choose **Format, Text Style** from the **menu bar**.

Click

2 Choose Import New Styles

In the **Text Style** dialog box, choose **Import new styles**.

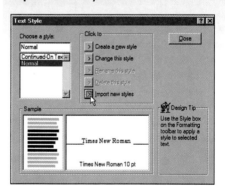

3 Double-Click to Import

When the **Import Styles** dialog box appears, make sure the **Files of type** field is set for **Publisher Files** (which is the default). Then move to the folder where you keep your publications and double-click the file that has the styles you want to import.

4 Copy Styles to Current Publication

All the styles that exist in the selected publication are copied to the current publication.

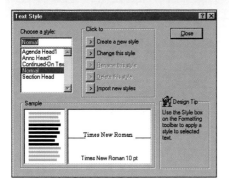

5 Check Imported Style

Check each imported style by looking at it in the **Sample** box. (It's common to find that the color scheme of an imported style doesn't match the color scheme of the current document.) If everything is fine, choose **Close** to import the styles.

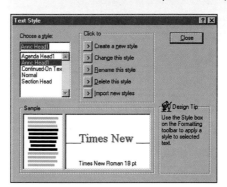

6 Changing Imported Styles

If you need to adjust the style for the current publication, choose **Change this style**. When the **Change Style** dialog box opens, select the appropriate category to effect your changes. For instance, to change color, select **Character type and size**. Choose **OK** to return to the **Text Style** dialog box, and then choose **Close** to import the styles into the current publication.

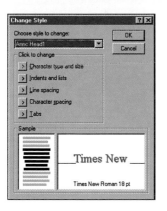

7 Applying Imported Styles

Now you can use the **Style** box on the **Text Formatting** toolbar to apply your newly imported styles to your publication.

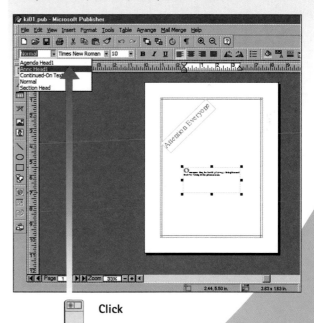

Click

End

How to Import Styles from Word Processors

Most of us use word processing software, and you may have created or tweaked some styles in your word processor that you'd like to use in Publisher. You can! You can import styles from your word processing documents to take advantage of all that special formatting.

The important thing to remember is that you're not importing styles from the word processing software, but that you're importing styles from a specific document that was created in that software. Of course, once you understand this, you should open your word processor and create a document that has all sorts of styles.

Begin

1 Load Publication Needing Styles

Load the publication that needs the styles into your **Publisher** window. Then choose **Format, Text Style** from the **menu bar**.

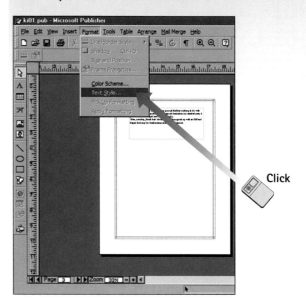

Click

2 Importing the Styles

In the **Text Style** dialog box, choose **Import new styles**.

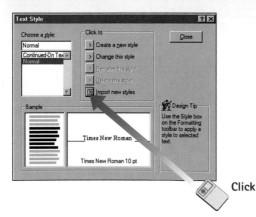

Click

3 Locate Your Word Processor

When the **Import Styles** dialog box appears, click the **arrow** next to the **Files of type** field to see the list of supported word processors. Select your word processor.

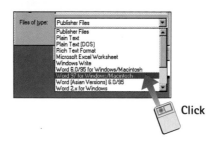

Click

4 Locate Your Document

Use the toolbar to move to the folder in which you save your word processing documents. Select the document that has the styles you want to import and choose **OK** (or double-click the **Document** icon).

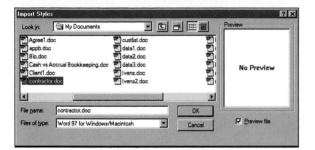

5 Delete Unnecessary Styles

The **Text Style** dialog box now displays all the styles that were attached to the document you chose. Examine the styles you're importing. Choose **Delete this style** to remove any you don't need. You may want to tweak one or more of the styles to make them more useful in Publisher. You can accomplish that by choosing **Change this style** and making the necessary alterations.

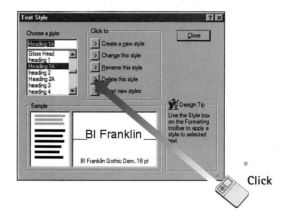

Click

6 Apply Styles to Publication

Choose **Close** to close the dialog box and import the styles. Then use the **Style** box on the **Text Formatting** dialog box to apply the style to the text in your publication.

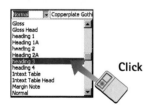

Click

End

How-To Hints

Add More Templates to Get More Styles

If you use Microsoft Word, you can continue to attach templates to a document; as you do, all the styles in those templates are added to the document template. This is a great way to get a lot of styles attached to one document.

Your Word Processor Must Be Supported

If your word processor isn't listed in the **Import Styles** dialog box (see Step 3), you cannot import styles.

How to Apply Formatting Quickly

Many times you'll create a terrific, complicated format for a particular section of text. Perhaps it's a heading or a fancy caption under a picture. You will probably want to use it again in the publication. In fact, you might want to use it many times, formatting all the text frames that hold similar text. This gives your publication a consistency that is slick and professional.

Begin

1 Click Format Painter Tool

Select the text frame you've formatted to the point of perfection. Then click the **Format Painter** tool on the **Standard** toolbar.

2 Position Mouse Pointer in Frame

Your mouse pointer turns into a paintbrush. Move to the text frame you want to format in and position your mouse pointer anywhere in the frame.

3 Click to Apply Formatting

Click to apply the formatting to the target frame.

4 Formatting Other Frames

If the target text frame is on the same page as the original text frame, right-drag (use your right mouse button to drag) the original text frame over the target text frame.

6 Formatting Multiple Frames

If you want to apply the formatting to multiple frames, select the original frame and choose **Format, Pick Up Formatting** from the **menu bar**.

5 Using the Apply Formatting Menu

When you release the mouse button, a menu appears. Choose **Apply Formatting Here**. Voilà!

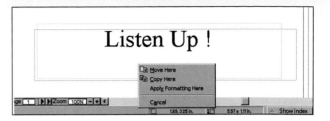

7 Reformatting Frames

Move through your publication and select the first frame you want to reformat. Choose **Format, Apply Formatting**. Repeat for each target frame in your publication.

End

How-To Hints

Create a Style from Your Formatting

Most of the time, this sort of ultra-distinctive formatting is specific to the publication. If you create a formatting example that is useful for many publications, consider turning it into a style. See Chapter 2, Tasks 10 and 11 for information on creating styles and importing them into other publications.

How to Format Text Frames

In addition to formatting the text that resides in your text frames, you can format the frame itself. This adds to the eye-catching appeal of frames and is especially effective for headings, captions, and short lists.

Begin

1 Colorizing the Frame

Select the frame to begin decorating it. You can preformat the text that's in the frame or wait until you've formatted the frame. To colorize the frame, click the **Fill Color** icon on the **Text Formatting** toolbar.

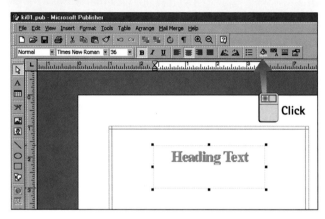

Click

2 Choose More Colors

Only a few color choices appear on the **Fill Color** menu, so choose **More Colors** to see a larger palette.

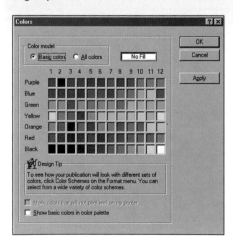

3 Adding Depth/Texture to Text Frames

To add depth, texture, or both to the look of the frame, choose **Fill Effects** from the **Fill Color** menu. Then either select **Patterns** to add an interesting textured background, or select **Gradients** to add a more subtle feeling of depth.

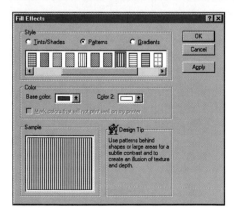

4 Aligning Text in a Frame

To position the text that's in the frame, choose **Format**, **Align Text Vertically**, and then choose an alignment pattern from the menu.

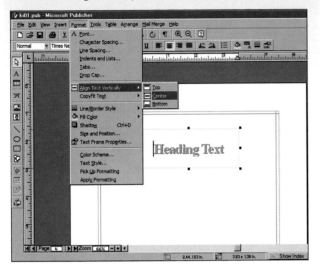

5 Adding Shadows to a Text Frame

Press **Ctrl+D** to add a shadow to the text frame. (It's a toggle, so if you change your mind, press **Ctrl+D** again.)

6 Adding Borders to a Text Frame

Click the **Line/Border Style** icon on the **Text Formatting** toolbar to select a quick border from the drop-down menu.

7 Formatting Borders

Choose **More Styles** from the **Line/Border Style** drop-down menu to configure a border with the settings you prefer. While you're there, look at the **BorderArt** tab, where you find fancy, artistic borders you might want to add to the frame.

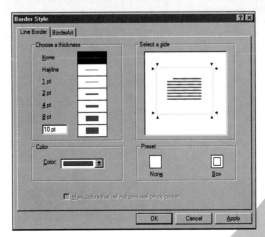

How-To Hints

Plan for Black-and-White Printing

It's tempting to add all sorts of colorful formatting gizmos to text frames, but remember that colors print as shades of gray when you don't have a color printer. That rich, deep, green background you add may print as such a dark gray that your black text disappears.

End

Task

Working with Graphics

Part of the fun of working in Publisher is adding graphics to your publication. It's a chance to be creative, innovative, and original. Text creation is full of rules such as spelling and grammar, but graphics offer an opportunity to do whatever you want to do, in any manner you prefer.

However, the robust graphics tools built into Publisher aren't there just so you can have a few moments of enjoyment; they serve a real purpose. You can use graphics to help emphasize the message in your text or to send a message independently, without text. Graphics help you produce a publication that's slick and attractive.

In this chapter you learn how to access graphics and then tweak them into a state of absolute perfection. ●

How to Insert Standard Shapes

Publisher 98 provides some preset graphic shapes, called standard shapes, and there are a gazillion uses for them. You can put text on them, pile them on top of each other to create pictures, or just add a splash of color to your page.

These standard shapes are the oval/circle, square/rectangle, and line. Publisher calls them *standard shapes* to differentiate them from a group of other shapes called *custom shapes* (which are covered in the following pages).

Begin

1 Select Oval Tool Button

To place an oval shape into your publication, click the **Oval Tool** icon on the **Objects** toolbar.

Click

2 Create Oval by Dragging

Drag your mouse to create the oval, stretching it as much as you want. You can also click the page to let Publisher insert the oval with a preset size and shape.

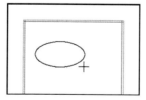

3 Create a Circle with Shift Key

To create a circle, follow the instructions in Steps 1 and 2, but hold down the **Shift** key as you drag the oval shape.

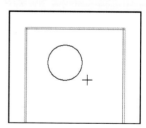

4 Select Rectangle Tool Button

Click the **Rectangle** tool on the **Objects** toolbar to create a rectangle or a square.

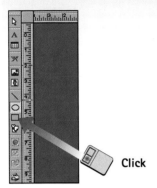

Click

5 Create Rectangle by Dragging

Position your mouse where you want the rectangle to start; drag to create.

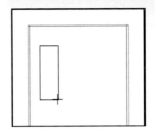

6 Selecting the Line Tool

To draw a line, click the **Line** tool on the **Objects** toolbar.

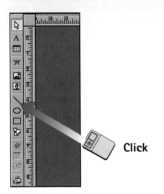

Click

7 Creating a Line by Dragging

Position your mouse where you want one end of the line; drag to create a line of the proper length.

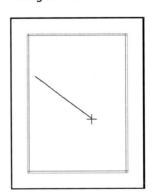

End

How to Insert Custom Shapes

Wait until you see the custom shapes in Publisher! As soon as you look at all the choices, your creative genes will go on full alert. The possibilities are endless, and you'll probably start inventing headlines and snappy phrases just to have a reason to use some of these shapes.

The real fun with custom shapes comes with "creative mouse dragging." You can manipulate your mouse as you're creating these shapes to produce weird and unusual graphics.

Begin

1 Select Custom Shapes Tool

Click the **Custom Shapes** button on the **Objects** toolbar.

Click

2 Select a Shape

The assortment of custom shapes displays. Click the shape you want to work with.

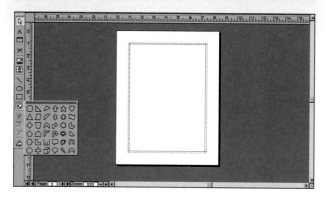

3 Drag Mouse to Create a Shape

Drag your mouse to create a custom shape in the size and proportion you require. It's best to drag diagonally in order to maintain a reasonable facsimile of the original shape.

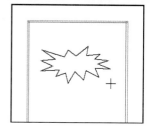

4 Hold Shift Key for Proportional Shapes

To keep the shape's form as you create it (which means you don't change its proportions), hold down the **Shift** key while you drag.

5 Drag Mouse for Disproportional Shapes

On the other hand, it's fun to distort a shape for a special effect. Just drag the mouse disproportionately, more downward or to the side than diagonally.

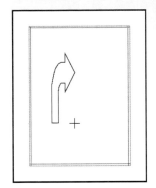

6 Click to Simply Insert Shape

You can select a shape and then click your page to insert the shape in its default size. The center of the shape is placed at the location of your mouse pointer when you click.

End

How to Move and Resize Shapes

Luckily, if you're not an accomplished "mouse dragger," you can tweak and correct the appearance and size of a shape after you've inserted it in your publication. In fact, the ability to manipulate shapes after they're placed on the page means you can click to insert a shape instead of dragging it.

Begin

1 Select a Shape

Click the shape to select it. When an object is selected, sizing handles appear around it.

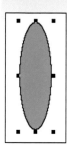

2 Position Mouse Pointer Over Shape

Position your mouse pointer anywhere over the shape. Your pointer turns into a moving van.

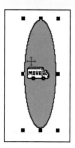

3 Move Shape to New Location

Press and hold the left mouse button to move the shape to another location.

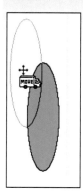

4 Position Mouse on Size Handle

Position your mouse pointer on a sizing handle to see the pointer turn into a **resize** pointer.

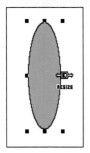

5 Drag to Resize

To resize the shape, press and hold the left mouse button and drag the resizing handle in the appropriate direction. Because you're working with shapes, this also changes the shape's appearance.

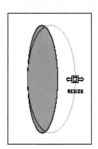

6 Control Key for Proportional Resize

To force an equal movement on the opposite side as you resize, hold down the **Ctrl** key while you drag a resizing handle. (Actually, what's happening is that the center of the shape is being forced to remain where it is.)

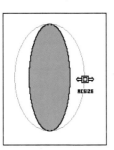

7 Use Corners to Resize Two Sides

To resize two sides at once, use the corner sizing handles. Notice that even round shapes have corner sizing handles.

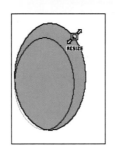

End

How-To Hints

Stop Mid-Stream if You Need To
If you're dragging a resizing handle and change your mind, just press the **Esc** key to cancel the action.

How to Add Color and Texture to Shapes

Most shapes, especially the standard shapes, need some help before they add much to your publication. The thin outline of a shape isn't much of an attention getter.

You can add pizzazz to your page by changing the look of a shape, which is quite easy to accomplish.

Begin

1 Click a Shape

Click a shape to select it.

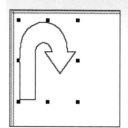

2 Click Fill Icon

To add color to the shape, click the **Fill Color** icon on the **Formatting** toolbar.

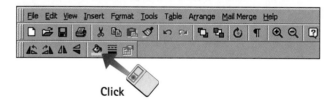

Click

3 Change a Color

The **Fill Color** menu displays the colors that make up the color scheme for this publication. The bottom line of color swatches displays any colors you've recently used (which makes it easy to use the same colors throughout the publication). Click a color swatch to fill the shape with that color.

4 Choose More Colors

Choose **More Colors** from the menu to see a full palette. Select the color you want to use and choose **OK**.

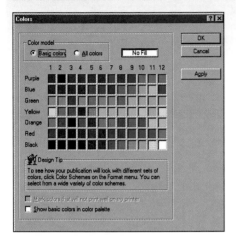

5 Choose Fill Effects

Choose **Fill Effects** from the **Fill Color** menu to add patterns or texture to your shape with the **Fill Effects** dialog box. Select **Patterns** and then scroll through the available patterns to pick the one you like. Don't forget to select a color. (You can select a second color to have the pattern lines colorized.)

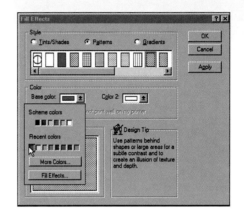

6 Choose Gradients

Select **Gradients** to fill your shape with a color that has an air-brushed effect. Pick the gradient pattern you like and select a color. Choose a second color to put behind the gradient.

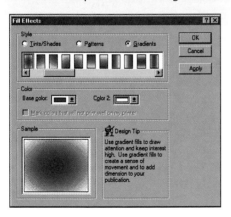

7 Tweak to Perfection

Check the effect, and if you have to tweak the colors or fills, repeat these steps until everything looks terrific.

End

How to Layer Shapes

One of the nifty things you can do with shapes is put them together to make entirely new shapes. You can stack them or overlap them to create interesting graphics.

There's a trick to all this, however, because layering automatically occurs according to the order in which the shapes are placed on your page. The first shape you create is on the bottom of a layer (even if you aren't layering). Then each additional shape assumes its position in the next higher layer.

1 Create Some Shapes

Create the shapes you want to put together.

2 Select and Drag a Shape

Select a shape and drag it in order to put it on another shape.

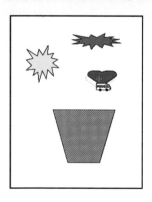

3 Notice One Shape Disappears

Uh oh. The shape is still selected (you can see the sizing handles), but it has disappeared behind the shape it's supposed to sit upon.

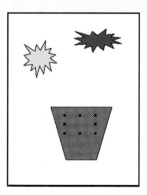

4 Choose Bring Forward

If you have more than two shapes, you might want to layer a shape on top of one shape, but not all the way to the front. (Perhaps you don't want the flower petals to cover the heart decoration.) To move shapes through the layers by degrees, choose **Bring Forward**.

5 Press F6 For Quick Layering

Bring a shape to the front layer quickly by selecting it and pressing the **F6** key.

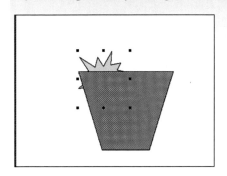

6 Press Shift F6 for Back Layering

Send a shape to the back layer quickly by selecting it and pressing **Shift+F6**. In this case, the line that is supposed to be the stem is selected.

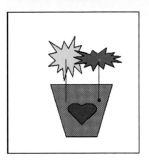

End

How-To Hints

Layers Work the Same Everywhere
The rules for layering apply to all types of frames in Publisher; it's just easiest to illustrate it with shapes.

How to Put Text on Shapes

One of the best uses you can make of a shape is as a background for important text. The shape draws the reader's eye and adds zest to your page.

Begin

1 Click Text Frame Tool

Create the shape and add color or texture to it. Then click the **Text Frame** tool on the **Objects** toolbar.

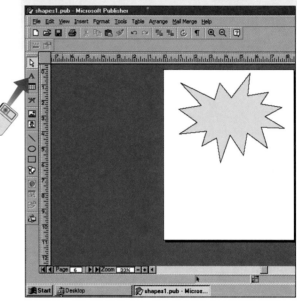

Click

2 Create a Text Frame

Drag your mouse to create a text frame that fits in the shape.

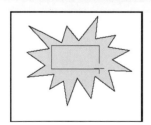

3 Enter Text in Frame

Enter the text in the text frame. (It's easier to work if you press **F9** to zoom in.)

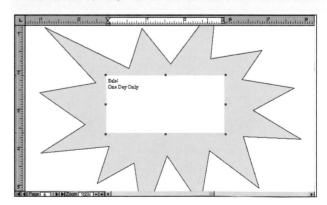

4 Format Text

Format the text. Usually it's a good idea to center text in a shape.

5 Zoom Out with F9 Key

Press **F9** to zoom out. Click anywhere outside the page to deselect the objects on the page so you can see the effect.

6 Press Ctrl+T for Transparent Frame

To make the text frame transparent (so that it looks as if the text were directly on the shape), select the text frame and press **Ctrl+T**.

7 Color or Texturize Frame

If you want to use the text frame for additional color or effect, select it and add color or texture.

End

How-To Hints

Where to Go for More Information

See Task 4 in Chapter 3, "How to Add Color and Texture to Shapes," on page **90–91**.

See Task 2 in Chapter 2, "How to Resize and Move Text Frames," on page **56–57**.

See Task 4 in Chapter 2, "How to Format Text Appearance," on page **60–61**.

How to Insert Clip Art

Clip art is a picture, usually a simple line drawing with lots of color. Publisher 98 provides an enormous collection of clip art in the Clip Gallery, and you can open the gallery when you need an illustration.

Because the collection is so large, the majority of the clip art files are kept on the Publisher 98 CD-ROM. When you want to select clip art, you must make sure the CD-ROM is in its drive.

Begin

1 Click Clip Gallery Tool

Click the **Clip Gallery** tool on the **Objects** toolbar. Drag your mouse to create a frame of the right size on the page where you want to insert the clip art, or click the page to let Publisher insert the frame. (You can resize it later.)

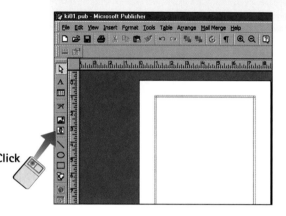

Click

2 Opening MS Clip Gallery

The Microsoft Clip Gallery opens as soon as you release the mouse.

3 Insert the Clip Art

Find the clip art image you want to use and double-click it.

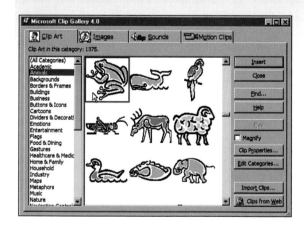

4 Moving/Resizing Clip Art

The clip art image is placed in its frame on your page. You can move it or resize it as you need to.

6 Enter Search Term

In the **Find Clips** dialog box, enter a descriptive word for the type of clip art you need. You can enter multiple words to narrow the search, separating each word with a space. You can also narrow the search to a particular category. Choose **Find Now** to begin the search.

How-To Hints

Use Categories to Save Time

It's much easier to find appropriate clip art if you select a category to reduce the number of images you have to scroll through.

5 Reselecting Clip Art

To change the clip art that's currently in the clip art frame, double-click anywhere on the frame to reopen the Clip Gallery. To find an appropriate illustration, click the **Find** button on the **Clip Gallery** window to search for specific types of illustrations.

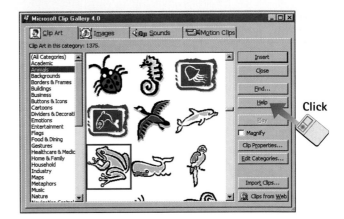

Click

7 Insert the Clip Art

The gallery displays all the clip art that matches your criteria. (It invents a category called **Results of Last Find**.) Scroll through the images and double-click the clip art you want to use.

End

How to Insert Pictures

The Clip Gallery has pictures in addition to clip art, and sometimes one of these photographs provides exactly the illustration you need. If you have pictures from any source available as a file, such as scanned images or downloaded artwork, it's easy to insert them into your publication.

Begin

1 Create A Clip Art Frame

Click the **Clip Gallery** tool on the **Objects** toolbar. Drag your mouse pointer to create a clip art frame, or click the page to let Publisher create the frame.

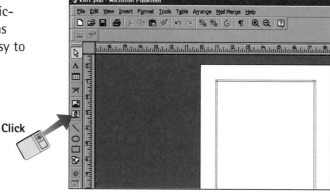

Click

2 Double-Click Clip Art

When the Clip Gallery opens, move to the **Images** tab. Double-click the picture you want to use to insert it in the frame.

3 Click Picture Frame Tool

To insert a picture file that's not clip art, click the **Picture Frame** tool on the **Objects** toolbar.

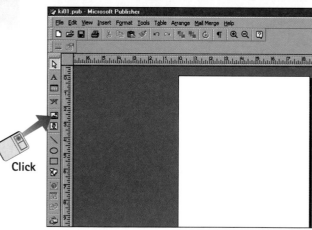

Click

4 Create Frame and Insert Picture

Drag the frame to the size you need. Then choose **Insert**, **Picture** from the **menu bar**. Choose **From File** to select a picture file from your hard drive.

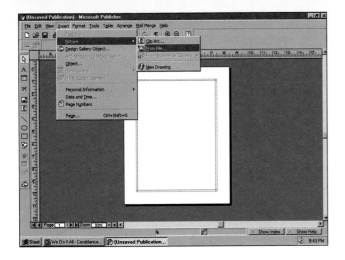

5 Double-click to Insert Picture

When the **Insert Picture File** dialog box opens, the pictures that were installed to your hard drive by Publisher are displayed. (They're from the clip art collection.) Click a file to see a preview in the **Preview** box and choose the one you want.

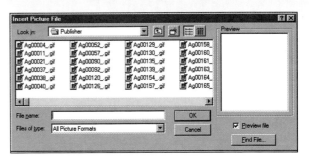

6 Find Other Pictures on Hard Drive

To use other pictures (perhaps you've scanned pictures or received picture files from friends), move to the folder where you keep picture files and double-click the one you want to use.

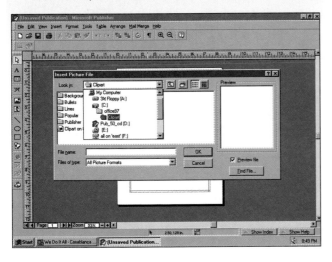

7 Moving/Resizing Pictures

Move or resize the pictures as necessary, but be careful not to distort the image (unless you deliberately want the effect of distortion).

End

How to Insert WordArt

WordArt is a way to bend and twist text and graphics, and it's lots of fun! You enter text, but Publisher treats the frame as a graphic.

Begin

1 Click WordArt Frame Tool

Click the **WordArt Frame** tool on the **Objects** toolbar.

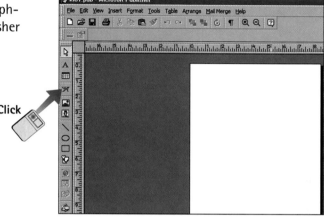

Click

2 Create a Frame

Drag to create a frame of the right size.

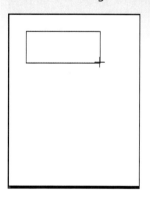

3 Release Mouse

When you release the mouse, a **WordArt** text frame is on the page, and the **Enter Your Text Here** dialog box sits in front of it.

4 Enter Text in WordArt Frame

Enter your text in the dialog box. (Just start typing; your characters replace the selected text automatically.) Keep the text short; this is not a place for long sentences.

5 Click Update Display

Choose **Update Display** to transfer the text to the **WordArt** frame. Then close the dialog box by clicking the **X** in the upper-right corner. The **WordArt** frame has a hash-mark look, which means it is in WordArt edit mode.

6 Edit WordArt Frame

To edit the frame (or to move or resize it) instead of the WordArt, click outside the frame to deselect it. Then click anywhere in the frame to select the frame. The familiar sizing handles appear to indicate the frame is selected.

7 Edit WordArt

To edit the WordArt text, double-click anywhere in the frame. The hash-mark frame and the **Enter Your Text Here** dialog box appear so you can change the text. Close the dialog box so you can format the WordArt text (which is covered in the following pages).

End

How to Format WordArt

Now the fun starts. Formatting WordArt is a cheery, amusing activity. Even better, the results add real pizzazz to your publication. Remember that there are two ways to select a WordArt frame:

- Single-click to select the frame, so you can move or resize it.

- Double-click to put the WordArt text into edit mode, so you can change the text or format it.

Click outside the WordArt frame to deselect either selection mode. When you are in edit mode, the **WordArt software application** window is on your screen. When you deselect the frame, you return to the **Publisher 98** window. The problem with the **WordArt** window is that the **Formatting** toolbar has no **ScreenTips**, so you have to pay careful attention to the information on these pages to understand all of the buttons.

2 Pick a WordArt Shape

Click the **arrow** to the right of the **Style** box to reveal the available shapes for WordArt. Pick a shape and your text twists to match the shape, which is referred to as *pouring* your text into the shape.

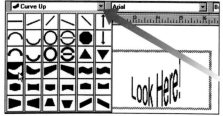

Click

Begin

1 Select WordArt Frame

Double-click the **WordArt frame** and then close the **Enter Your Text Here** dialog box by clicking the **X** in the upper-right corner. The frame is bordered with hash marks.

Look Here!

3 Change WordArt Font

Sometimes pouring the text into a shape makes it a bit more difficult to read. Usually you can fix that by changing the font, so click the **arrow** next to the **Font** box and select a font that works better. You can also change fonts because you feel like it. (It's part of the fun of WordArt.)

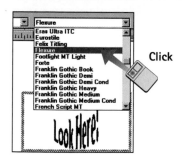
Click

4 Change Letter Size

The **Font Size** box is configured for **Best Fit**, and even though you can click its **arrow** to change the font, you find that **Best Fit** almost always fits best. In addition, the **Best Fit** font size changes automatically if you resize the **WordArt** frame.

Click

5 Format WordArt Text

Use the **Bold** and **Italic** buttons to format the text. Use the **Even Height** button to make lowercase letters the same height as uppercase letters.

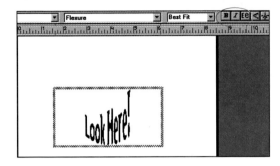

6 Flip Text

Click the **Flip** button to change the direction of your text.

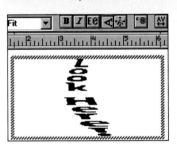

7 Stretch Text

Stretch the text with the **Stretch** button.

Continues

How to Format WordArt Continued

There's no end to the twists, turns, and other manipulations you can apply to the text in your **WordArt** frame. Here are some more examples of the formatting choices available:

Some of the choices involve the spacing of characters, specifically tracking and kerning.

Tracking is the amount of space between characters.

Kerning is the automatic adjustment of the space between certain pairs of characters, where the second character in the pair can easily be tucked in under (or next to) the first character. An example is any lowercase letter following a *w*, because you can move the letter under the right slant of the *w*.

9 Change Letter Spacing

Click the **Character Spacing** button to change the way the characters are laid out. Specify your selection in the **Spacing Between Characters** dialog box.

8 Align Text with Frame

Click the **Alignment** button to reposition the text's relationship with the frame.

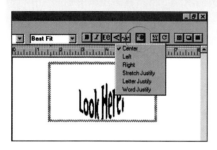

10 Rotate Text

Click the **Special Effects** button to rotate or skew the text. Use the **Rotation** box to specify the number of degrees you want to rotate the WordArt. Use the **Slide** box to type a percentage of skewing. A **50%** value is used as the norm. Anything under 50% skews text to the right, and anything over 50% skews text to the left. In effect, you're changing the shape that holds your WordArt.

11 Add Texture

Click the **Shading** button to add texture or patterns to the text. This is unusual; most of the time you add fill (texture or patterns) to frames, not text. However, you must single-click the frame and then use the tools on the **Graphics Formatting** toolbar to add fill in WordArt.

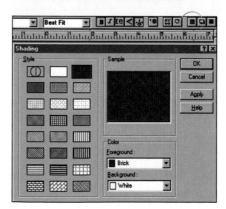

12 Add Shadow

Click the **Shadow** button to add a drop shadow to the text. The **Shadow** dialog box presents an interesting variety of choices. You can also select a color for the drop shadow. Always make the shadow color a lighter version of the text color; usually **Silver** works best, regardless of the color of the text.

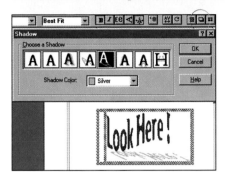

13 Add a Border

Click the **Border** button to add a border to your WordArt text (again, not the frame). If you add a border, it won't be seen unless you choose a different color.

14 Deselect Frame

Deselect the frame to check the effect as you work.

End

How to Use Microsoft Draw

Microsoft Draw is automatically installed with Publisher 98, and you can use it while you're working in Publisher. As you see in these pages, it launches automatically and disappears when you're finished working on your **MS Draw** frame.

MS Draw creates frames that have multiple objects. There are lots of nifty tools and graphics you can use to create complex graphic frames, and you can even make your own drawings.

Begin

1 Select Picture Frame Tool

Start by selecting the **Picture Frame** tool on the **Objects** toolbar.

2 Create New Frame

Drag to create a frame and then choose **Insert, Picture, New Drawing** from the **menu bar**.

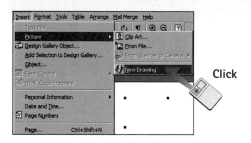

Click

3 Add Elements to Your Frame

Now you're working in Microsoft Draw. The **AutoShapes** toolbar floats in the window so you can add elements to your frame.

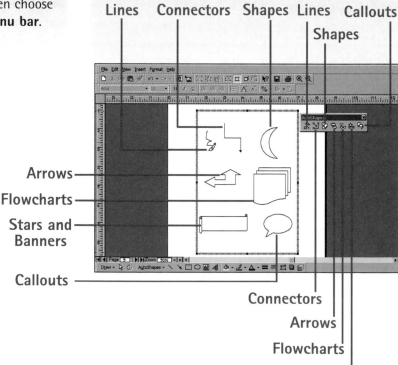

Lines Connectors Shapes Lines Callouts

Shapes

Arrows

Flowcharts

Stars and Banners

Callouts

Connectors

Arrows

Flowcharts

Stars and Banners

4 Select an Element

Select an element to work with it. Different types of elements provide different types of editing opportunities. For example, select a shape and right-click to see the options on the **shortcut menu**.

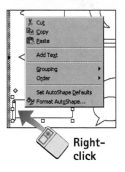

Right-click

5 Choose Add Text

Choose **Add Text** from the **shortcut menu** to place text on a shape. You don't need to add a text frame, just type directly on the shape.

7 Using Format AutoShape

All the elements offer the **Format AutoShape** option on the **right-click menu**. The dialog box offers lots of options. (The **Picture** and **Text Box** tabs are grayed out if you haven't inserted those elements in the shape.)

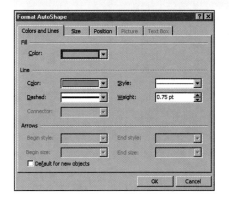

6 Click Insert Clip Art or Picture

To use a shape as a frame for additional elements, select the shape and then click the **Insert Clip Art** or **Insert Picture from file** button on the **Standard Formatting** toolbar.

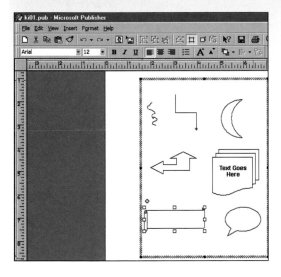

End

How-To Hints

Draw Has Its Own Help

When you're working in Microsoft Draw, there's an independent Help system you can use to become more adept with this application.

Toggling Between Publisher and Draw

To leave Microsoft Draw and return to your **Publisher** window, click anywhere outside the Microsoft Draw object. Double-click the object to return to Microsoft Draw.

How to Create Borders and Shadows

After your graphic is nestled nicely in its frame, you might want to decorate the frame a bit. A plain border makes the graphic stand out, separating it from the other frames on the page.

A shadow or a decorative border around the frame adds even more luster to your graphic image. This can add to the aesthetics of the frame and also directs the reader's eye to the contents.

Begin

1 Select Graphic Frame

Click the **graphic frame** to select it. The **Graphics Formatting** toolbar appears in the **Publisher** window.

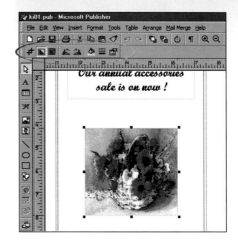

2 Click Line/Border Style Button

Click the **Line/Border Style** button on the **Graphic Formatting** toolbar.

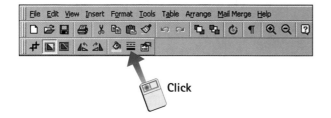

Click

3 Select a Line

Select one of the lines in the **drop-down menu** to put a simple border around the frame.

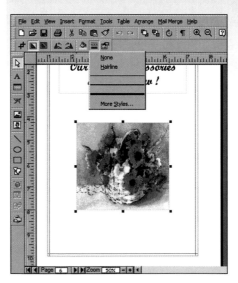

4 Select More Styles

For additional choices, choose **More Styles** to open the **Border Style** dialog box. You can select any thickness or change the bottom choice (by default, 10 points) to specify any point value. You can also choose a color if you want one.

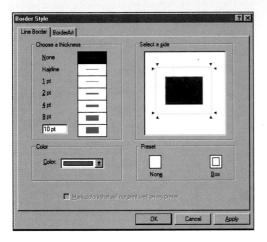

5 Creating a Shadow

Create a shadow by holding down the **Shift** key as you click on any two adjacent sides in the **Select a side** section of the dialog box. You can also create a border by placing different-sized borders on sets of sides. (Use **Shift+Click** to deselect any selected side; the clicking action is a toggle.)

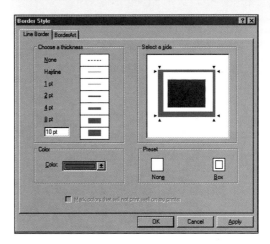

6 Choose a Border

Move to the **BorderArt** tab and scroll through the selections to find a decorative border that suits the graphic. You can adjust the width of the border by specifying the points in the **Border size** box.

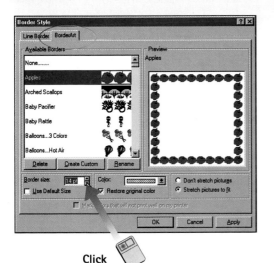

Click

7 Apply Your Border

Choose **OK** to close the dialog box and apply your border.

End

How to Group and Ungroup Objects

After you put a text box on a shape, a caption under a picture, or a graphic in a text frame, what do you do if you have to move all that stuff around?

It's a real chore to move the shape and then move the text box, replacing it in exactly the same position. In fact, resizing a frame that has something on it or in it means you also have to resize the interior frame to keep the proportions correct.

Luckily, Publisher has a feature that makes all of this easier. You can group objects together and then manipulate the group. What you do to one you do to all. This can save hours of work and frustration.

Begin

1 Lasso Objects to Group

Drag your mouse to lasso the objects you want to group. This creates a virtual box around the elements. (If your box crosses an object but doesn't completely encompass it, that object won't be included in the group.)

2 Hold Shift to Select and Group

Alternatively, you can select multiple elements by holding down the **Shift** key as you click each object.

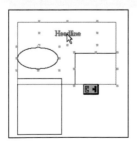

3 Group Objects Button Appears

A frame appears around all the objects in the group and a **Group Objects** button is displayed at the bottom of the frame. The group exists temporarily (until you click anywhere outside the group) and you can manipulate it as a single unit.

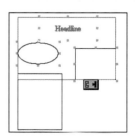

4 Click Group Objects Button

Click the **Group Objects** button to make the group permanent. The button and buttonhole come together.

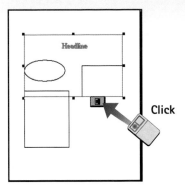

Click

5 Move Group

To move the group, position your pointer over any element in the group and drag to bring all the objects along.

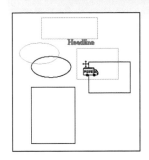

6 Resize Group

If the group is permanent (the buttonhole is closed), sizing handles appear around the group frame. When you resize the group, each element in the group changes its size proportionately.

7 Format Group

You can also apply formatting changes to the group, such as colorizing or rotating the frames.

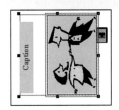

8 Deselect Group

Ungroup the objects by clicking the **Group Objects** button. Then click anywhere outside the group to restore the individual frames.

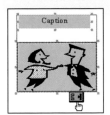

End

How to Align Objects

Frames that are associated, such as captions and pictures or groups of like items, need to be positioned so that the association is obvious. Additionally, lining up a page's elements in an orderly fashion makes your publication look much more professional.

You can align objects to margins or to each other, depending on the effect you want to produce. Each alignment action must be performed individually, which means that if you want to line up one group of objects in one way and another in a different way, you must perform two sets of steps.

Begin

1 Select Objects

Select each of the sloppily arranged objects by holding down the **Shift** key as you click each element.

2 Choose Align Objects

Choose **Arrange**, **Align Objects** from the **menu bar**.

Click

3 Align Objects Vertically

In the **Align Objects** dialog box, use the **Left to right** section of the dialog box to align objects that are positioned vertically on your page. If you want to line up the objects along their frame edges, specify the edge you want to use and choose **OK**.

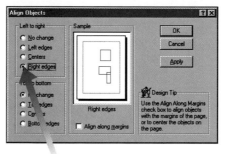

Click

4 Align Objects Horizontally

Use the **Top to bottom** section of the dialog box to align objects that are positioned horizontally on your page.

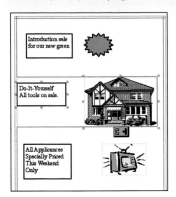

5 Align in Relation to the Margin

Select the **Align along margins** option to line up the elements in relation to the margins instead of in relation each other. If you choose an edge, the closest margin is used as a guide. If you choose **Center**, the objects are centered between the margins.

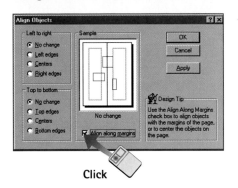

Click

6 Aligning in Columns

Here you have columns of objects. After you align them vertically, you usually have to repeat the process to align them horizontally.

End

How-To Hints

Align Edges for Columns

It's easier to read and understand columns of objects if you align associated items so that their top or bottom edges are on the same line, instead of centering them.

How to Use the Snap To Feature

For a professional look, all the pages in your publication should have objects lined up in a similar manner. The element at the top of the page should be in the same place on each page. Columns should have their edges in the same place. Full-page text frames should have the same margins on every page. You can drive yourself nuts moving objects around your pages or aligning them one page at a time—or you can let Publisher do it for you automatically.

To accomplish this, you need to insert guide lines. Turn on the Snap To feature to place virtual magnets on your objects and the guide lines. As soon as they get close to each other—*bang!*—they line up together.

Rulers provide **Snap To** lines for individual pages where objects should line up in a certain position on the page. Layout Guides provide **Snap To** lines for the entire publication.

2 Dragging Ruler into Position

Continue to hold down the **Shift** key as you drag your pointer to the position on the page where you want to insert a **Snap To** ruler guide. (Don't worry, the green line on your screen doesn't print.) Repeat for as many ruler guides as you need.

Begin

1 Creating a Ruler Guide

To create a ruler guide, hold down the **Shift** key and position your pointer on either ruler. Your pointer turns into an **Adjust Pointer**.

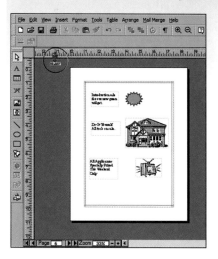

3 Create a Layout Guide

To create a Layout Guide you must work on the background page so that the guide line is repeated on every page. Press **Ctrl+M** to move to the background page. The **status bar** replaces your page number with a **background page** icon.

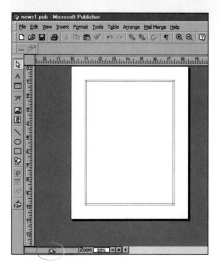

4 Choose Layout Guides

Choose **Arrange**, **Layout Guides** from the **menu bar**.

Click

5 Specify Number of Columns/Rows

In the **Layout Guides** dialog box, create a grid with the guide lines you need; do this by specifying the number of **Columns** or **Rows** (or both) it takes to line up all the elements in your publication. Choose **OK** and then press **Ctrl+M** to leave the background page.

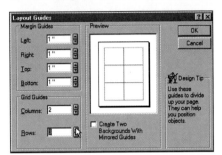

6 Turn on Snap To

Make sure the Snap To features you need are enabled on the **Tools** menu. A **check mark** indicates that the feature is enabled.

Click

7 Drag Objects to Guidelines

Drag an object toward the appropriate guide line. When you get close, it snaps to the guide line automatically.

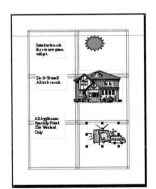

End

How to Wrap Text Around Graphics

If you want to illustrate a story or article, the illustration should be inserted in the story. This makes your publication far more professional, because when you do this, the text automatically moves and rewraps itself to make room for the illustration. The resulting look is called *text wrap*.

Begin

1 Select an Illustration

Create a graphic frame, perhaps adding **Clip Art**, inside the text frame. (Select the **Clip Art** tool and insert an illustration.) Click the illustration for the frame.

2 Text Rewraps Automatically

The text rewraps automatically around the graphic frame. The text uses the edge of the frame as a margin.

3 Click Object Frame Properties

To force the text to wrap around the picture itself instead of the frame, select the **graphic frame** to put the **Graphics Formatting** toolbar in the window. Then click the **Object Frame Properties** tool.

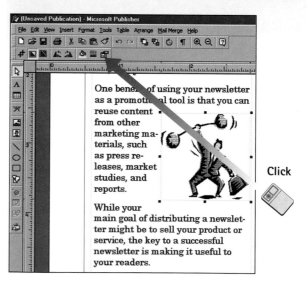

Click

4 Select Picture Only

In the **Object Frame Properties** dialog box, select the **Picture Only** option; then choose **OK**.

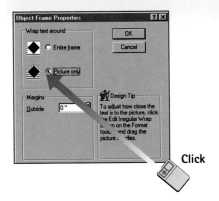

Click

5 Click Irregular Edit Wrap Button

The text rewraps, using the picture itself as a margin. This frequently causes a spillover of words onto the wrong side of the picture.

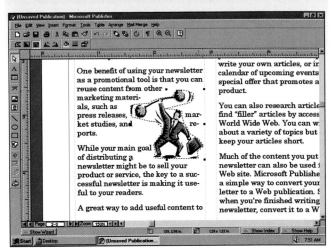

6 Tweak the Margins

To tweak the picture's margins (and therefore the text wrap), click the **Edit Irregular Wrap** button on the **Graphics Formatting** toolbar.

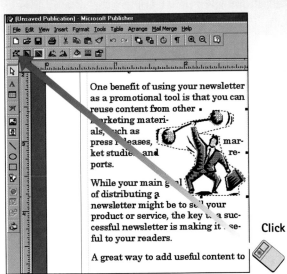

Click

7 Resize Picture's Margins

Sizing handles appear everywhere there is a bend or a curve in the picture. Drag the appropriate sizing handles to fix the text wrap problem.

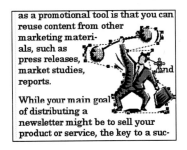

End

How-To Hints

Don't Wrap Text on Both Sides

Don't place a graphics frame in the middle of text; it forces the text to wrap on both sides of the illustration. Readers will have to skip over the illustration to complete each sentence—a terribly annoying way to read.

How to Move, Resize, and Crop Graphic Frames

As you work on a publication, you'll find you are constantly rearranging, tweaking, and changing the elements. That's part of the quest for perfection.

Most of your graphics frames can be manipulated without incurring real harm to the general sense of your publication. When you work with text frames, you can't chop a bunch of words out of a sentence or move a couple of sentences to a different location—but graphics are usually more flexible.

Begin

1 Select the Frame

To manipulate a graphics frame, select the frame. (You can tell it's selected when you can see the sizing handles.)

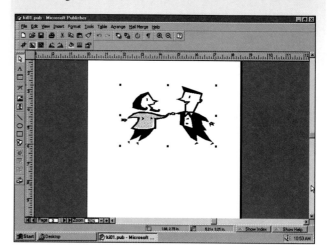

2 Move the Graphic

To move the graphic, position your mouse pointer anywhere in the frame. Your pointer turns into a **moving van**. Press and hold the left mouse button and drag the frame in the appropriate direction.

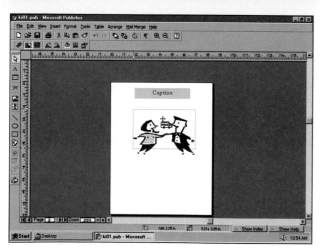

3 Making Fine Adjustments

If you're making a fine adjustment, you can nudge the frame instead of dragging it. Hold down the **Alt** key and press the appropriate **arrow** key. You can control the distance the frame moves with each nudge by choosing **Arrange**, **Nudge** from the **menu bar** and specifying a measurement in the **Nudge by** box.

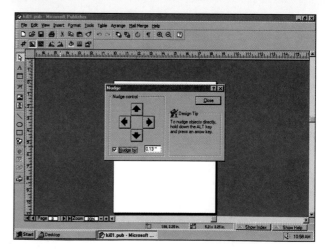

4 Resizing A Frame

Drag a sizing handle to resize the frame. Use a corner handle to drag two sides at a time.

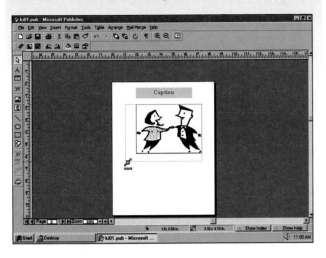

5 Resizing Proportionally

To resize the opposite side (or corner) by the same amount, hold down the **Ctrl** key as you drag.

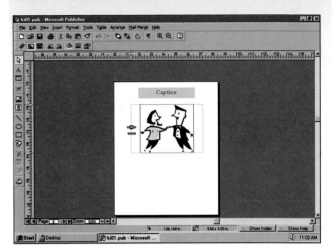

6 Cropping a Picture

To *crop* (cut away parts of) a graphic image, click the **Crop Picture** button on the **Graphics Formatting** toolbar. Position your pointer over a sizing handle to have the pointer turn into a cropping tool. Drag your mouse to enclose the portion of the picture you want to keep.

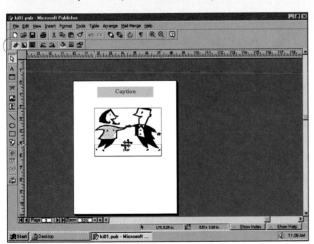

7 Cropping Other Sides

If necessary, repeat the cropping action on another side of the frame. Your pointer remains a cropping tool until you click the **Crop Picture** button again to turn cropping off.

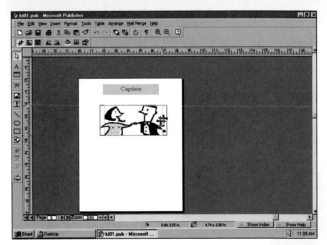

End

How-To Hints

Shapes and Cropping
Shapes cannot be cropped.

How to Flip and Rotate Objects

One of the many fun things to do when creating a publication is to turn frames topsy-turvy. Apart from being fun to do, you can use the results as eye-catching graphics. This is a nifty way to draw attention to a message.

You can rotate all graphics and text frames. You can flip shapes and WordArt. To rotate a frame 90 degrees left or right, click the appropriate button on the **Formatting** toolbar.

Begin

1 Rotating a Frame 90 Degrees

Select the frame you want to manipulate by clicking it.

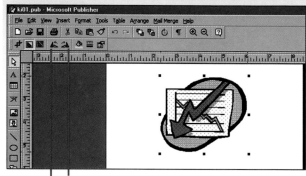

Rotate   Rotate
Left   Right

2 Press Alt to Rotate Manually

To control the rotation manually, hold down the **Alt** key and position your pointer over a sizing handle. The pointer becomes a rotation tool, and you can drag to rotate the frame.

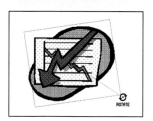

3 Choose Arrange

To rotate a frame by a specific number of degrees, choose **Arrange**, **Rotate or Flip**, **Custom Rotate** from the **menu bar**.

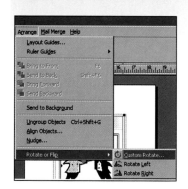

4 Specify Number of Degrees

Specify the number of degrees in the **Angle** box of the **Custom Rotate** dialog box.

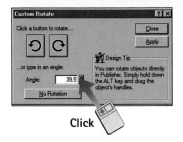

Click

5 Flip a Shape Horizontally

To flip a shape horizontally, select it and then click the **Flip Horizontal** button on the **Graphics Formatting** toolbar. The shape swivels as if you had moved it with a hinge running along either side.

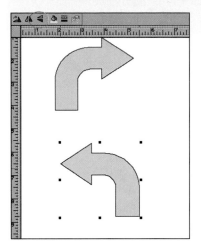

6 Flip a Shape Vertically

To flip a shape vertically, select it and then click the **Flip Vertical** button on the **Graphics Formatting** toolbar. The shape swivels as if you had swung a hinge attached to its top or bottom edge.

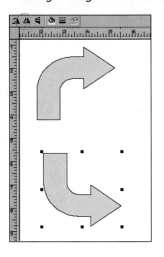

7 Flip WordArt

To flip WordArt, double-click the **WordArt** frame and click the **Flip** button on the **WordArt Formatting** toolbar. Be aware that flipped WordArt tends to be a bit strange and may be hard to read. You should probably adjust the font and character spacing. You can learn more about using WordArt in this chapter's Task 10, "How to Format WordArt."

End

How to Create Picture Captions

Captions are short phrases that describe illustrations. Sometimes you use a caption to explain a graphic, and other times you can use a caption to add to the message of a graphic that's very much self explanatory.

It doesn't really matter where you position the caption in relation to the graphic—there's no absolute rule about whether the caption should be above, below, or next to its illustration. Well, that's not always true—captions for cartoons are traditionally below the cartoon.

Begin

1 Create a Text Frame

Create a text frame above, below, or next to the graphic frame.

2 Enter Text

Enter your text and format it.

Our annual accessories sale is on now !

3 Move the Text Frame

Move the text frame, the graphic frame, or both, to put them as close together as possible.

4 Click Text Frame Properties Button

Click the text frame to select it and then click the **Text Frame Properties** button on the **Text Formatting** toolbar.

5 Reduce the Margin

In the **Text Frame Properties** dialog box, reduce the margin for the edge of the frame closest to the graphic. Choose **OK**. (This brings the text closer to the graphic frame.)

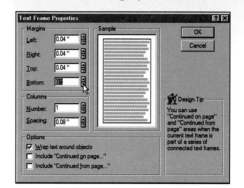

6 Group the Frames

Group the frames by holding down the **Shift** key as you select each frame or by drawing a line around both frames.

7 Click Group Objects Button

Click the **Group Objects** button on the bottom of the group frame to make the group permanent. Now if you move the picture, you also move the caption (and vice versa).

End

How-To Hints

Learn More About Text Formatting

You can learn about working with text frames and text in Chapter 2. Look for these titles:

Task 1, "How to Create a Text Frame"

Task 2, "How to Move and Resize Text Frames"

Task 3, "How to Enter Text and Use the Text Formatting Toolbar"

Task 4, "How to Format Text Appearance"

Project

Project 1

Here's a chance to use the skills you're acquiring as you work in Publisher 98. I'm going to build a publication (a fund-raising brochure), using the Publisher features and functions discussed in Chapter 1, "Getting Started," through Chapter 3, "Working with Graphics."

You can follow along, and if you prefer to use your own words and graphics, that will work just fine. This is a chance to put everything you've learned to work.

1 Open Publisher

Open Publisher by choosing **Programs, Microsoft Publisher 98** from the **Start** menu.

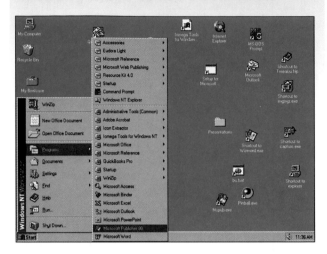

2 Expand Brochures List

Publisher opens with the Catalog in the software window; the **Publications by Wizard** tab is in the foreground. Click **Brochures** in the left pane to expand the list of brochures the wizard can build.

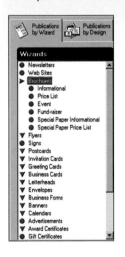

3 Select a Brochure

Select a brochure (I'm choosing Fund-raiser) and the right pane of the Catalog displays your selection's available publications. Select the one you want to use. A border surrounds your selection.

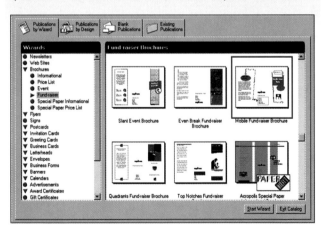

4 Start Wizard

Click **Start Wizard**.

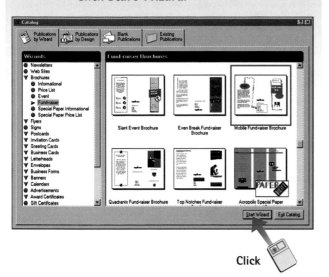

Click

5 Answer the Wizard's Questions

The wizard builds the layout for your publication. Your window's left side has the **wizard's panel**, which is where questions are presented, so you can choose the options for your publication. Click **Next** to begin answering the wizard's questions.

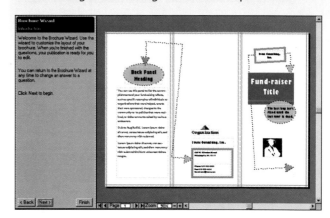

6 Choose a Color Scheme

The first wizard question is about the color scheme you want to use. The color scheme attached to the publication you chose in the Catalog is preselected, but you can click any other scheme in the **wizard** panel. Click **Next** when you've made your decision.

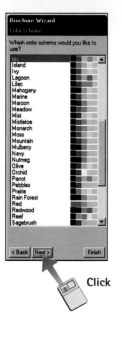

Click

7 Finish Up

Keep answering questions and clicking **Next**. When you've answered the last query, the **Next** button is inaccessible; click **Finish**.

Click

Continues

Project Continued

8 List Option Categories

The **wizard** pane lists all the option categories. Click any category to open that **wizard** pane if you want to change any of your decisions. (The wizard will redraw your layout when you make changes to your options.)

9 Hide the Wizard

The **wizard** pane is taking up room in your software window, so click **Hide Wizard**. If you need to make further changes, click **Show Wizard** to return this pane to your software window.

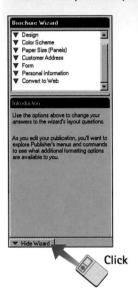

Click

10 Select Placeholder Text

The wizard has inserted placeholder text to indicate where you should enter your own message. Click anywhere in a text frame to select (*highlight*) all the placeholder text.

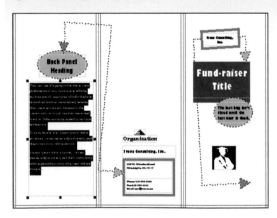

11 Enter Your Own Text

Press **F9** to zoom in to the text frame so you can see what you're typing and begin entering your text. As soon as you begin typing, the placeholder text is deleted.

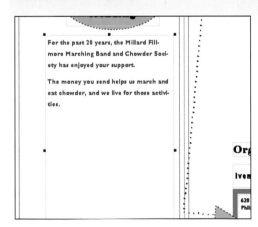

12 Save Your Work

It's time to save your work. In fact, it's a good idea to save every time you complete an individual task. Then, if something happens to the power (or your computer), the worst that can happen is that you lose the work you entered since the last time you saved. Click the **Save** button on the **Standard** toolbar.

Click

13 Name Your Publication

The first time you save a publication, the **Save As** dialog box displays so you can enter a name for your file. Publisher adds the extension **.pub** automatically, so enter a name and then click **Save**. (The Publisher software window's title bar now displays the filename.) By the way, if you've made changes to your publication since the last time you saved it, Publisher will remind you to save your work every 15 minutes.

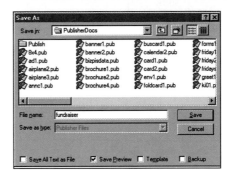

14 Zoom Back Out

Press **F9** to zoom back out and select another frame to work on. In this case, I want to put a different picture in a picture frame. Notice that when you position your mouse pointer anywhere on the frame a ScreenTip indicates the type of frame.

15 Select the Picture Frame

Click the picture frame to select it. Notice that handles appear around the frame when it's selected. In addition, your mouse pointer turns into a **moving van** to indicate that you can drag this frame to a different position.

Continues

16 Open the Clip Gallery

Double-click the frame to open the Microsoft Clip Gallery. Select a category from the left pane and then scroll through the right pane to find a picture you want to use in your publication. When you find the perfect illustration, double-click it to insert it in the picture frame.

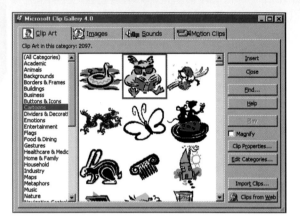

17 Resize a Frame

Change the size of the frame by placing your mouse pointer over one of the sizing handles, which turns your pointer into a **Resizer**. Drag the handle to enlarge or reduce the frame. (Use a corner handle to resize a graphics frame proportionately.)

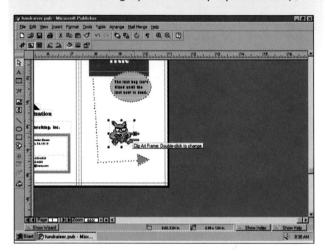

18 Change the Text Font

Select another frame to work on. In this case I'm selecting a text frame. To change the appearance of text, select the text and use the tools on the text **Formatting** toolbar. You can change the font by clicking the arrow to the right of the **font** box and selecting a different font.

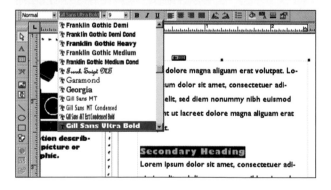

19 Make Text Bold or Italic

Change the text's attributes by clicking the **Bold**, **Italic**, or **Underline** button on the **Formatting** toolbar.

20 Change Text Alignment

Change the alignment of the text by clicking the appropriate alignment button on the **Formatting** toolbar (**Left**, **Center**, **Right**, or **Justify**).

21 Add a Border

To put a border around a frame, select the frame and then click the **Line/Border Style** button on the **Formatting** toolbar. You can add a border quickly by selecting one of the lines on the **drop-down menu**. To add color to the border or to use BorderArt (artistic borders), click **More Styles** and then make your selections in the **Border Style** dialog box.

22 Have Fun

Continue to select frames and add your own words and graphics to the placeholder elements. Use the tools on the **Formatting** toolbar to enhance the appearance of your publication. Have fun designing your masterpiece.

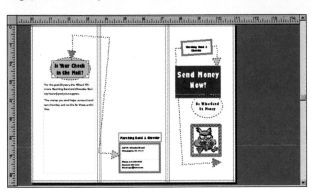

End

Task

4

Adding Special Elements

To make your publication even more professional and more interesting to readers, Publisher offers some fascinating features and tools.

You can use these tools to add elements to your publication that would be terribly difficult (or, in some cases, impossible) to create from scratch while you're working in Publisher.

Whether you need a stunning, eye-catching design or a complicated spreadsheet that was developed in another software program, Publisher makes it easy to add special elements to your publication.

In this chapter you learn about a number of these special features. ●

How to Add Symbols, Arrows, and Fancy Lines

There are all sorts of special characters available to you. Some of them are practical, others are used to create an eye-catching spot on a page, and some are just for fun.

Symbols are text, even though they don't look like any character in the alphabet. They exist within several fonts. (The font most famous for symbols is Windings, which has nothing but symbols in the font characters.)

Arrows and fancy lines are *graphics*.

Begin

1 Locate Symbol You Want to Insert

To insert a symbol in a text frame, position the insertion point at the spot within the text where you want the symbol to appear. Then select the frame and choose **Insert**, **Symbol** from the **menu bar**. The **Symbol** dialog box opens with all the characters available in the font that's currently selected. Scroll through the characters to find the symbols. You can also use the **Font** box to change the font in order to see different symbols.

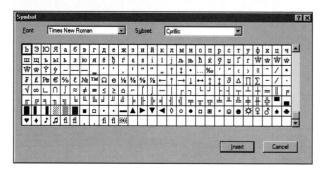

2 Double-Click the Symbol

Double-click the symbol you want to insert in your text frame. You can then format it, change the font size, and generally treat it as you do all other text. See Chapter 2's Task 4, "How to Format Text Appearance."

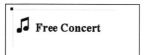

3 Creating an Arrow

To draw an arrow, click the **Line** tool on the **Objects** toolbar. Drag to create a line of the length you need. To keep the line straight and true, hold down the **Shift** key as you drag.

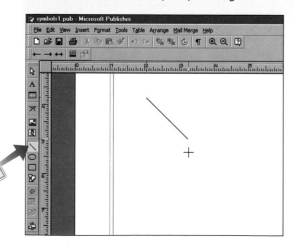

Click

4 Select the Appropriate Arrowhead

Click the line to select it (unless the line is already selected, as it would be immediately after you drew it). When a line is selected, **arrowhead** buttons appear on the **Formatting** toolbar. Click the button that matches the direction you want the arrow to point (left, right, or both ways). To make the arrow thicker, select a thicker line from the **Line/Border Style** button on the toolbar.

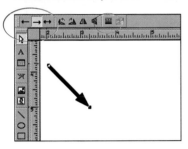

5 Creating a Fancy Line

To create a fancy line to separate frames or sections of text, click the **Rectangle** tool on the **Objects** toolbar. Drag a rectangle that's wide and thin.

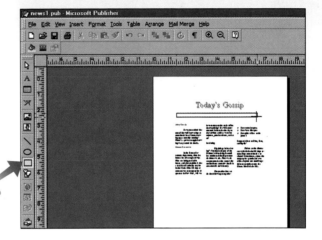

Click

6 Select a Style for Your Border

Click the **Line/Border Style** button on the **Formatting** toolbar and choose **More Styles**. In the **Border Style** dialog box, move to the **BorderArt** tab. Select the design you want to use for your line and choose **OK**.

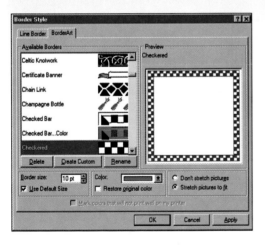

End

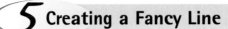

How-To Hints

Common Symbols

Symbols you should become familiar with include the variety of fractions available and special characters for inserting dashes. In publishing there are two dash characters used, the em dash (usually as wide as the letter M) and the en dash (half the width of the em dash). Use the em dash to separate phrases in a sentence. Use the en dash to separate a range such as "Read pages 1–3."

How to Add a Table

A table is a terrific way to present lists of information, and you probably have lots of publications in which this type of information has to be presented.

Begin

1 Create a Frame

Click the **Table Frame** tool on the **Objects** toolbar. Drag to create a table frame of the size you need.

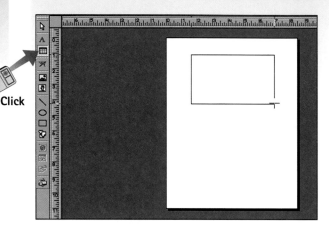

Click

2 Specify the Number of Rows/Columns

When you release the mouse, the **Create Table** dialog box opens so you can configure the table. Start by specifying the **Number of rows** and **Number of columns**.

3 Pick a Table Format

Scroll through the **Table format** list to find the layout design that fits your table. The **Sample** box shows you what the format looks like.

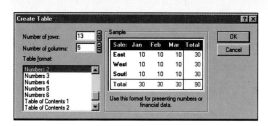

4 Resize Table If Necessary

If the size of the frame you dragged isn't large enough to hold the number of rows and columns, Publisher offers to resize the table. Of course, you should accept the offer by clicking the **Yes** button.

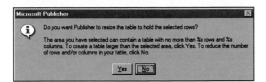

5 Enter Data into the Cells

Enter data and use the **Tab** key to move between cells. (Use **Shift+Tab** to move backward.)

Name	Number of Vacation Days	Number of Days Used	Number of Days Remaining	Seniority Number for Picking Days

6 Format the Data in the Cells

Each individual cell is a text frame, and you can use the tools on the **Text Formatting** toolbar to change the text's appearance.

End

How-To Hints

Other Things to Read

For more information about formatting frames, read Task 14, "How to Format Text Frames," in Chapter 2.

How to Format a Table

You can tweak a table to make it look interesting, attractive, and slick. You can merge cells, add rows or columns, and create borders.

Because a table is a collection of text boxes (*cells*) arranged in rows and columns, the formatting changes you make can be applied to a variety of elements:

- You can change the formatting of an individual cell or a group of selected cells.
- You can change the formatting of a row, a column, or the entire table.

Some of the common formatting changes for tables include the following:

- Format the row that holds titles for center alignment.
- Format columns that contain numbers for right alignment.
- Merge cells to create title rows at the top of the table or a total row at the bottom.

Begin

1 Use Table AutoFormat to Change Table Appearance

To change the basic appearance of the table, click anywhere in the table to select it and choose **Table**, **Table AutoFormat** from the **menu bar**. Choose a new design.

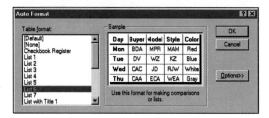

2 Merging Cells

To merge cells (in order to create one cell from multiple cells), select the cells you want to merge and choose **Table**, **Merge Cells**. You can select cells by dragging your mouse across them, holding down the Shift key while you press an arrow key, selecting a column or row selector (the shaded area next to a row or above a column), or by clicking in the first cell, then clicking in the last cell while you hold down the Shift key.

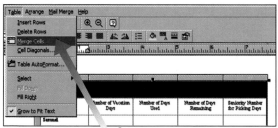

Click

3 Formatting Columns and Rows

To change the formatting for a column or row, click the column or row selector. (A column is selected here.) Then use the tools on the **Formatting** toolbar to apply changes such as alignment, color, fill, or font.

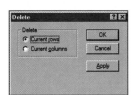

4 Adding Columns or Rows

To add rows or columns, click anywhere in the row or column adjacent to the new addition. Then choose **Table**, **Insert Rows or Columns** from the **menu bar**. In the **Insert** dialog box, specify how many new rows or columns you want to add and where they should be placed.

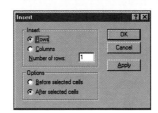

5 Removing Columns or Rows

To remove rows or columns, click anywhere in the row or column you want to get rid of and choose **Table**, **Delete Rows or Columns** from the **menu bar**.

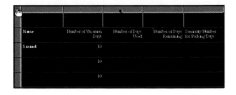

6 Auto Fill Data in Cells

To fill in data automatically (for data that is the same in multiple cells), select the first cell that has data inserted and drag your mouse to select the cells below or to the right to which you want to copy the data. Choose **Table**, **Fill Down** or **Fill Right** to copy the data.

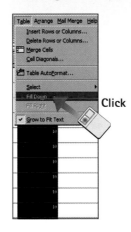

7 Formatting the Entire Table

To make a formatting change to the entire table quickly, select the table by clicking the table selector (the gray box in the upper-left corner). Use the tools on the **Formatting** toolbar to apply changes such as alignment, color, fill, or font.

End

How to Use the Design Gallery

There's a little art gallery tucked into Publisher 98, and you can visit it to pick up fancy art work that enhances your publication. The Design Gallery's options cover a wide range of design types, from generic (things like ornamental graphics) to specific (calendars, coupons, and order forms).

Some of the designs can be dropped into your publication without any additional work. Other designs, such as calendars and coupons, require configuration and perhaps some text entry. All the designs have wizards if you don't want to make changes manually.

Begin

1 Click the Design Gallery Toolbar

Click the **Design Gallery Object** button on the **Objects** toolbar.

Click

2 Review Designs in the Design Gallery

When the Design Gallery opens, the **Objects by Category** tab is in the foreground. The window's left pane lists the categories, and when you select a category the available designs are displayed in the right pane.

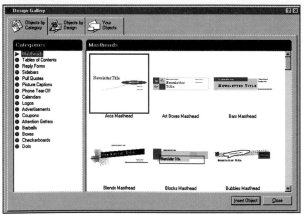

3 Click the Objects by Design Tab

Click the **Objects by Design** tab to see the designs available there. The left pane displays a list of the designs; as you select a design you'll see a variety of objects that use that design. This is a good way to make sure that important elements in your publication have the same look.

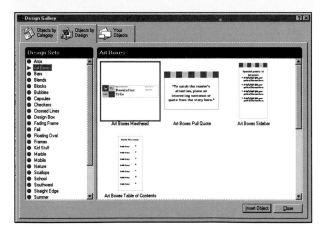

4 Select a Design Element

Select a design element and choose **Insert Object** to place it on your page (or double-click it).

5 Customize the Design Element

A button appears at the bottom of the design when the design is selected. Click the button to launch the wizard that's specific to this design. For most designs, the wizard merely permits you to change the design color scheme. For some, more complicated design elements (such as a calendar), the wizard helps you configure the design. Picking the month and year for a calendar is an example.

6 Customize the Illustration

If the design has an illustration and you want to substitute a different illustration, choose **Insert, Picture** from the **menu bar**. Choose the type of illustration you want to insert in the design from the **submenu**.

7 Customize Text

If the design has text (such as the attention-getter objects), select the text in order to replace it with your own words. To replace the text, you have to type words.

End

How to Create Your Own Design Gallery

The Design Gallery has a place where you can store the fancy stuff you've created on your own. Later you can open the gallery to use one of your own creations in the current publication or any other publication.

Just like the designs offered by Publisher, your designs must have a category and name. To make it easy, Publisher walks you through each step of placing your design in the gallery.

Your own designs are placed in the Design Gallery on a publication-by-publication basis; there is no way to save all the designs from multiple publications in one place. However, there is a way to get to a design from one publication while you're working in another one.

Begin

1 Select the Design Element

After you've created a magnificent design element on your own, select it. If it's made up of multiple elements (as are most of the Publisher designs in the gallery), create a group and select it.

2 Click Design Gallery Object Tool

Click the **Design Gallery Object** button on the **Objects** toolbar.

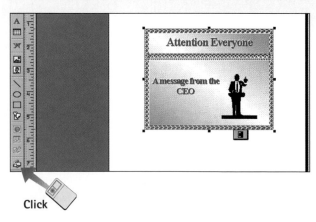

Click

3 Choose Add Selection To Design Gallery

When the Design Gallery opens, move to the **Your Objects** tab and click the **Options** button. Choose **Add Selection To Design Gallery**.

4 Enter Object's Name and Category

In the **Add Object** dialog box, enter an **Object name** and a **Category**. (As you continue to add designs to the gallery for this publication, you can use the category names you've already created.)

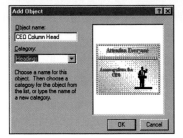

5 Inserting Your Design in the Same Publication

When you want to use this design element again in the same publication, open the Design Gallery and move to the **Your Objects** tab. Select the category and design you want to use.

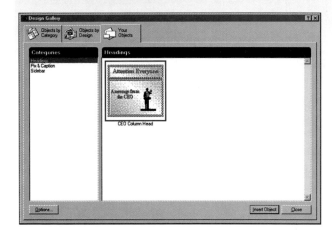

6 Inserting Your Design in a Different Publication

If you want to use your designs from one publication when you're working in another publication, open the Design Gallery and move to the **Your Objects** tab. Click the **Options** button and choose **Browse**.

7 Locate and Double-Click to Insert

In the **Other Designs** dialog box, select the publication that has your designs saved in its Design Gallery. Double-click it to open its designs in the Design Gallery; select the design you want to use.

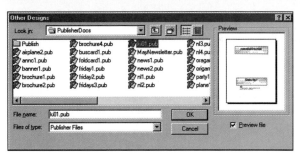

End

How to Create Background Elements

The publication's background page lurks behind the pages you use to create elements for your publication. There are two background page characteristics that make it an ideal location for page numbers, titles, company logo designs, and other elements that you want throughout your publication:

- You can place elements on the background page and they're visible when you work on the foreground pages. Of course, they're also visible when you print your publication.

- Whatever you place on the background page is seen on every foreground page.

Begin

1 Go to the Background

To work on the background page, choose **View**, **Go to Background** from the **menu bar**. The background page looks like a blank page, but there's a visual reminder on the status bar: The **background page** icon replaces the **page number** buttons.

2 Add Guidelines

The background page is also used for guide lines, which set margins and partition pages for your publication. These guide lines help you arrange and align objects not only in the background, but in the foreground, too. To create guide lines for your background page, choose **Arrange**, **Layout Guides** from the **menu bar**. When the **Layout Guides** dialog box appears, change margins or create grid lines as needed.

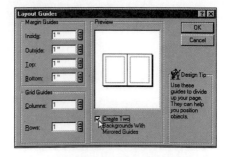

3 Create a Text Box for Page Numbers

To insert page numbers, create a text box in the appropriate position on the background page. To make sure the page number shows through, choose a position that's outside the margins you're using on the foreground pages.

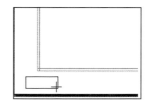

4 Insert Page Numbers

Select the text box and choose **Insert**, **Page Numbers** from the **menu bar**. Publisher inserts a pound sign (#) in the text box, which represents the code that it uses for the page number. (The actual page number appears on the foreground pages.)

Click

5 Format Page Numbers

You may want to add text (such as "Page") before the pound sign. You can also format the text and the page code using the tools available on the **Text Formatting** toolbar.

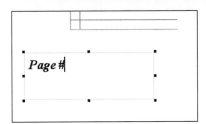

Page #

How-To Hints

Creating Two Background Pages

If your publication is printed on both sides of the paper and will be treated like a book, you can create two background pages. That means, for instance, that all the left pages can have numbers on the left side of the page and the right pages will print with numbers in one of the right-hand corners.

If your publication will be printed like a book and you want separate background pages, select **Create Two Backgrounds With Mirrored Guides** in the **Layout Guides** dialog box. Two **background page** icons appear on the **status bar**.

6 Repeat Page Number if Using Mirrored Pages

If you have mirrored background pages, move to the other page by clicking its icon on the **status bar** (unless you're working in a Two-Page Spread view, where you can scroll over to the other page). Repeat the procedure on the other background page, remembering to put the text box on the opposite corner. (Never use the inside edge of the page for a page number.)

Click

Continues

How to Create Background Elements Continued

In addition to text, you can add graphic images to the background page. For example, it might be nifty to have a splash of color on every page. Perhaps you could add some zest by putting a starburst or other graphic shape behind the page number.

7 Add Text Boxes to Publication

Create text boxes for any text you want to appear on every page of your publication. You can format the text on a background page in exactly the same way you format text on the foreground pages.

8 Add Graphics

To create a colorful graphic, create a shape on the background page. Some shapes lend themselves well to page numbers, chapter numbers, or other text. Place a text frame on the shape and make it transparent (**Ctrl+T**).

9 Click Clip Gallery

To create a picture watermark, click the **Clip Gallery** tool on the **Objects** toolbar.

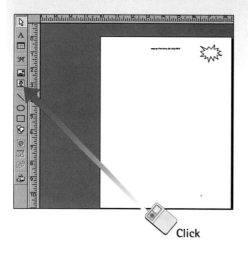

Click

10 Choose an Image

Select an appropriate graphic image in the Clip Gallery. Don't choose anything with a lot of detail or with colors that create the detail (watermarks are not multicolored). Click **Insert** (or double-click) to put the image on the background page.

Click

Double-click

11 Recolor the Image

Now that the graphic is on your publication's page, choose **Format**, **Recolor Object** from the **menu bar**.

Click

12 Choose Fill Effects

In the **Recolor Object** dialog box, click the arrow next to the **Color** box to see the drop-down menu. Choose **Fill Effects**.

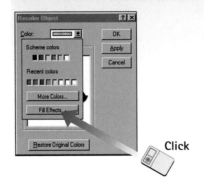

Click

13 Choose Light Gray

In the **Fill Effects** dialog box, choose a light gray color in the **Base color** box. (If light gray is not offered in the drop-down palette, choose **More Colors** to see the full palette.) Choose **OK** twice to close the dialog boxes and recolor the graphic.

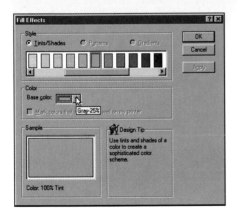

14 Press Ctrl + M

Choose **View**, **Go to Foreground** to return to the foreground page and check your work. If the watermark is hidden by the text frame, select the text frame and press **Ctrl+T** to make it transparent.

End

How-To Hints

Use WordArt for Text Watermarks

A *watermark* is a graphic, so if you want to use text within your watermark you must create a WordArt graphic. Learn more about WordArt by reading Chapter 3's Task 9, "How to Insert WordArt" and Task 10, "How to Format WordArt."

How to Insert Elements from Documents

It's not unusual to need data in your publication that's the same already entered in another software package. A report you wrote might belong in the company newsletter, or a spreadsheet might be needed for the annual report. Publisher provides a way to insert that information directly into your publication, so you don't have to spend time retyping it.

Publisher supports file types for most of the popular applications. (If you use Microsoft programs, you can be assured your data will import.) Check the Publisher documentation or contact Microsoft for an up-to-date list. For information on handling overflow text, see Task 8 in Chapter 2, "How to Work with Overflow Text."

Begin

1 Create a Text Frame

Click the **Text Frame** tool on the **Objects** toolbar and create a text frame to hold your imported document.

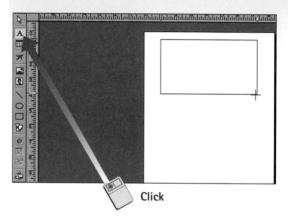

Click

2 Insert a Text File

Choose **Insert**, **Text File** from the menu bar.

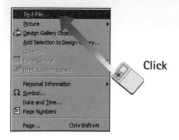

Click

3 Select the File You Need

When the **Insert Text File** dialog box opens, move to the folder on your hard drive that contains the document you need. Select the file by double-clicking it.

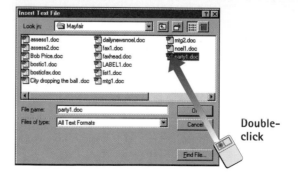

Double-click

4 Placing Excess Text

Very often the document is too large for the text frame you created. You can have Publisher automate the process of placing the excess text throughout your publication, or you can do it yourself.

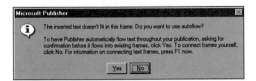

Microsoft Publisher

ⓘ The inserted text doesn't fit in this frame. Do you want to use autoflow?

To have Publisher automatically flow text throughout your publication, asking for confirmation before it flows into existing frames, click Yes. To connect frames yourself, click No. For information on connecting text frames, press F1 now.

[Yes] [No]

6 Publisher Imports a Spreadsheet

Publisher imports the spreadsheet and recognizes it, creating a table in your text frame.

	January	February	March	April	May	June
Week 1	250	226	320	421	501	498
Week 2	300	206	316	402	492	503
Week 3	250	220	339	396	459	480
Week 4	296	251	365	361	506	490
Average	274					

5 Importing Spreadsheet Documents

Spreadsheet application documents are imported in the same manner as text. (Publisher catches on, but you begin by using the **Insert, Text File** command.) When you select the spreadsheet document, Publisher wants to know if you want the entire document or a named range. (Click the arrows to select workbook sheets or named ranges.) Choose **OK** after you've made your selection.

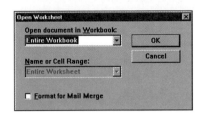

Open Worksheet

Open document in Workbook:
Entire Workbook   [OK]
                       [Cancel]
Name or Cell Range:
Entire Worksheet

☐ Format for Mail Merge

7 Using the Clipboard to Add Text to a Text Frame

You can also use the Windows Clipboard to move data into a Publisher text frame. Open the original software, select the data, and copy it. Move to your Publisher text frame and choose **Paste**.

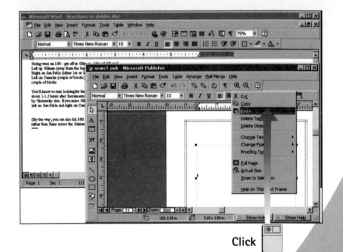

Click

End

How-To Hints

Using Database Reports

If you want to use reports from your database or accounting software, create those reports as disk files—be sure to specify the file type as text—then bring that text file into your word processor so you can import it into Publisher.

Using Parts of Documents

If you only need a portion of a document, select that portion in the document's original software program and save it as a separate document. In a spreadsheet document, create a named range. This is easier than bringing the whole document into Publisher and editing it there.

How to Use Mail Merge

There are a great many publications that are meant to be distributed by mail. Perhaps you create brochures, flyers, and price lists that must be mailed to customers. Perhaps you use Publisher at home and want to create your own holiday greeting cards or send a change-of-address notice. Publisher will print each individual mailing address on your publication so all you have to do is fold and stamp the paper.

To use Mail Merge, you must prepare the two main ingredients:

- The mailing list
- The publication, which is preset with codes to indicate where the various parts of the mailing address are printed (name, address, city, and so on)

Unlike the Mail Merge in database and word processing programs, Publisher can't use email address books. There are a limited number of lists Publisher can handle automatically (lists created in Access or Word usually work), but most of the time it's better to import lists into a Publisher address list or create a Publisher address list from scratch.

Begin

1 Create a Publisher Address List

To create a Publisher mailing list, choose **Mail Merge, Create Publisher Address List** from the **menu bar**.

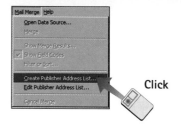

Click

2 Enter Information in Address List

The **New Address List** dialog box opens, and you can begin entering names, addresses, and other information.

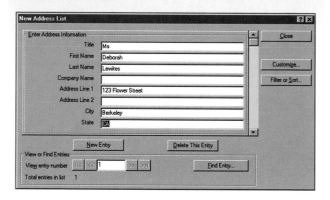

3 Choose New Entry or Close

Scroll down and enter any additional data you want to keep about this entry. Choose **New Entry** to save this addressee's information and bring up another blank screen so that you can type the next entry in the list. Choose **Close** when you are finished entering addressees.

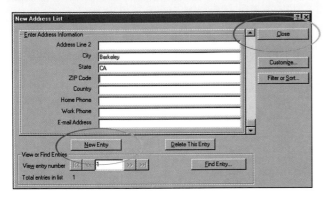

4 Save the Address List

In the **Save As** dialog box, give this mailing list a name and choose **Save**. (Publisher adds the .mdb extension to the filename automatically.)

5 Import an Existing Address List

To use a mailing list that exists as a database file, a Microsoft Word file, or a text file, first select the text frame that you are going to use for mailing; then choose **Mail Merge, Open Data Source** from the **menu bar**. When the **Open Data Source** dialog box appears, choose **Merge information from a file I already have**.

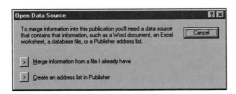

6 Specify Address List's File Type

The next **Open Data Source** dialog box appears so you can move to the appropriate folder to find your mailing list file. Specify the type of file you're seeking in the **Files of type** box. Double-click the file you want to use.

Continues

How-To Hints

You Need a Frame to Hold the Address

If you're planning to use Mail Merge to send your publication, remember to say **Yes** when the wizard asks if you want a placeholder for a mailing address.

How to Use Mail Merge Continued

After you've set up the mailing list you can begin inserting fields into your publication; *fields* are placeholders for the information that will be merged into each printed copy of the publication from the mailing list.

7 Answer Wizard Questions

Publisher usually has a few questions about how you want to use this file and how to recognize the information within it. Your answers depend on the type of file and its layout, which is information you should know before importing the list.

8 Create a Text Frame

After creating or importing your address list, open the publication into which you want the information from the list merged. (You can use the same list with any number of publications.) Select or create the text frame in which you want the Mail Merge information to appear.

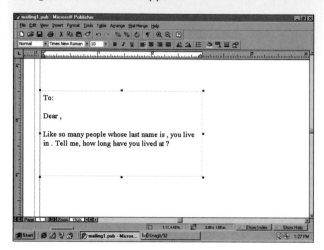

9 Select the List

Choose **Mail Merge, Open Data Source, Merge information from a file I already have**. On the dialog box that appears, choose the list file (the **.mdb** file) you saved earlier when you created or imported the list.

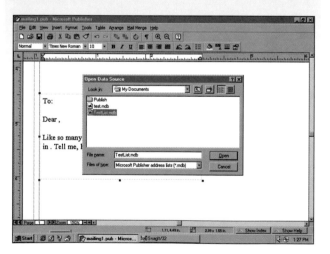

10 Attach the List to the Publication

The **Insert Fields** dialog box opens. Select a field—**First Name, Last Name**, and so on—and click **Insert**. The field name appears in the text frame, surrounded by double carats (<< >>). The field you see is a placeholder for the real information that will be inserted automatically in Step 10. After inserting a field, you may either insert another field or click **Close** to close the **Insert Fields** box. (To open it again to insert more fields, choose **Mail Merge, Insert Field**.)

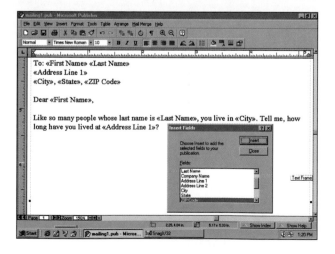

11 Merge the List

Choose **Mail Merge**, **Merge** from the **menu bar**. In the text frame you'll see the field names replaced by information from the first entry in the list. To examine the other entries in their place in the page, use the buttons on the **Preview Data** dialog box to move through your mailing list. Close the **Preview Data** box when finished previewing.

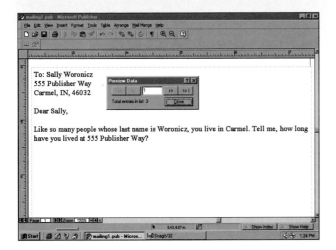

12 Print the Mail Merge

To print all copies of the publication, each containing one list entry's data in place of the field name placeholders, choose **File**, **Print Merge** from the **menu bar,** and then click **OK** on the **Print Merge** dialog box. Optionally, you can click **Test** on the **Print Merge** dialog box to print just one copy of the publication (showing just one list entry) to make sure that the Mail Merge data is formatted and positioned the way you want it without having to print the whole list.

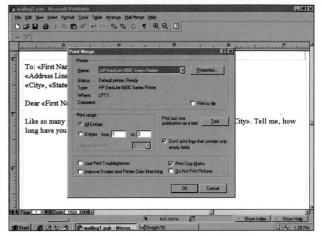

End

How-To Hints

Design Your Merge Text!

You can apply formatting—fonts, sizes, and so on—to the Mail Merge field names in the text frame. When you merge or print, the list data will be displayed or printed with that formatting.

Task

5

Tweaking Your Publication

There are publications and then there are PUBLICATIONS. The difference is measured in slickness, which is slang for "Hey, this really looks professional."

It's not an accident that magazines, newspapers, greeting cards, and other published documents look good enough to incite people to pay for them—a lot of attention is paid to detail.

Publisher has tools that help you pay the same amount of attention to detail, from the mundane chore of checking spelling to advanced tweaking techniques such as copyfitting.

You learn about these tools in this chapter.

How to Tweak Margins

Your publication is chock full of margins. There are margins for the page, the paper (not the same thing as the page), and each frame in the publication.

To give you one more thing to worry about, there are even margins for your printer. All laser and deskjet printers need to grab a small part of the paper in order to pull the paper through the printer. Nothing prints in that "grab" area.

Begin

1 Set Page Margins

To set the page margins for your publication, choose **Arrange**, **Layout Guides** from the **menu bar** to bring up the **Layout Guides** dialog box. Make the margins smaller to increase the amount of space you can use for printing.

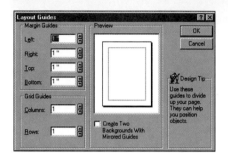

2 Set Page Margins for Background

To set the page margins for the background, press **Ctrl+M** to move to the background page. Then choose **Arrange**, **Layout Guides** from the **menu bar** to bring up the **Layout Guides** dialog box. Make the margins smaller to increase the amount of space you can use for printing. (Check your **Printer Properties** dialog box to learn the size of the unprintable area.) Learn about using the background in Chapter 4's Task 6, "How to Create Background Elements."

Control + m

3 Set Margins for Frames

To set margins for frames, select the frame and click the **Frame Properties** button on the **Formatting** toolbar, which opens the **Layout Guides** dialog box. By default, text frames have margins set; graphic frames (including WordArt) are set for no margin space. You can make changes to margins to alter the look of the frame.

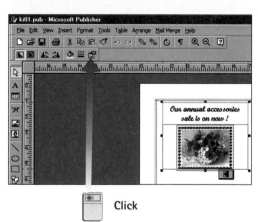

Click

4 Check Publication Size

Some publications are smaller than the paper that's used to print them. For example, a 5-inch by 7-inch flyer might be printed on 8.5-inch by 11-inch paper; the excess is trimmed away after printing. To check the publication size, zoom out to a zoom factor at which you can view the whole page, and then look at the **Rulers** to measure the publication. If the publication is smaller than the paper on which you will print it, you have the option of eliminating margins altogether and using *bleeds*, as described next.

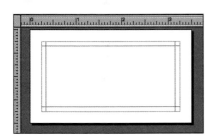

5 Creating a Bleed

If the page is smaller than the paper, you can set the margins that are not at the end of the paper to **0** (creating a bleed). Notice that the **Preview** box in the **Layout Guides** dialog box reflects your changes.

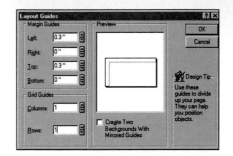

6 Creating Bleed Overruns

In fact, you can create frames that overrun the bleed edges. You can bleed color, but you must set the appropriate text margins to make sure you don't lose any characters.

7 Cutting Paper with Bleeds

When you print publications with bleeds, after you finish printing you must cut the paper. Sometimes this means the publication is a good candidate for outside printing services (where cutting is done automatically on machines).

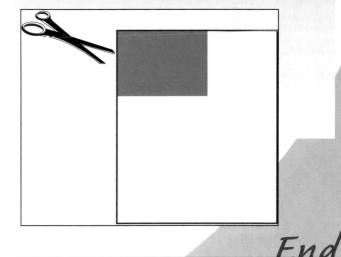

End

How-To Hints

Create Colors That Run to the Edge

You can print to the edge of your final page (after you cut to size) if your paper is larger than your page size. The stuff that prints past the margin is called *bleed*. This doesn't work, of course, for the publications that are designed to be the same size as your paper (8.5×11 inches). You can make it work by using an outside printing service that can handle larger paper.

How to Copyfit

Copyfitting is the art of fitting text into a specific amount of space. For years in advertising agencies, publishing houses, and printing companies the person who could compute the necessary copyfitting numbers was highly regarded. There were special rulers and guides (a circle with a slot on top of a background circle—you twirled the circles to compute the space you had available against the font sizes needed). In the face of computerized publishing, copyfitting as a manual task is becoming a lost art.

Begin

1 Hold Ctrl and Resize Frame

If a headline uses two lines and you prefer one-line headlines, try expanding the width of the text frame. Hold down the **Ctrl** key while you drag the sizing handle to change both sides at once.

2 Turn Bold On/Off

Very often, removing bold formatting from a headline copyfits the headline perfectly. The only difference between the two text frames shown here is that the **Bold** icon on the **Text Formatting** toolbar is clicked to toggle off the **Bold** attribute for the text in the top frame.

3 Reduce/Increase Font Size

You can also reduce the font size. If the text frame has a headline or a list, you can try reducing just one section of text to fit everything into your frame. Select the text you want to change and choose a new size from the **Font Size** box on the **Text Formatting** toolbar.

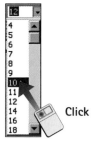

Click

4 Click Best Fit

To let Publisher copyfit the text frame automatically, select the frame and choose **Format**, **Copyfit Text**, **Best Fit**.

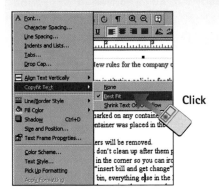

Click

5 Best Fit and Text Frames

As long as the check mark enabling the automatic copyfitting is present, Publisher continues to refit the text when you change the size of the text frame.

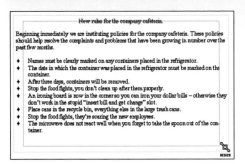

6 Best Fit and Font Size

In addition, changing the font size of any part of the text doesn't work when automatic copy-fitting is enabled—the text jumps right back to the size best suited for copyfitting.

7 Reducing Overflow Text

To make sure there is no overflow text in a text frame, choose **Format**, **Copyfit Text**, **Shrink Text on Overflow**. The automatic copyfitting goes into effect by reducing font size as soon as you type past the bottom of the frame into the overflow area. (Learn more about this in "How to Work with Overflow Text" in Chapter 2, "Working with Text.")

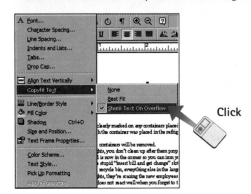

Click

End

How-To Hints

Don't Enlarge the Frame to Force Copyfitting

It's usually easier to solve a copyfitting problem for a single text frame by enlarging the frame, but if you do that often enough you'll end up having a great deal of trouble fitting all the text and graphics you need into your publication. The solution is to combine manual tweaking with the copyfitting tools and assistance that Publisher offers.

How to Control Tracking, Kerning, and Leading

You can control the way text fits and looks by changing the spacing. There are three ways to control spacing in publishing:

- Tracking—Changing the size of the spaces between characters.
- Kerning—Changing the size of spaces between specific pairs of characters. These pairs have special attributes when they exist, and they either look best squeezed together or separated.
- Leading (pronounced ledding)—Changing the spacing between lines.

Begin

1 Character Spacing Dialog Box

To change tracking or kerning, select the paragraph(s) you want to tweak and choose **Format**, **Character Spacing** from the **menu bar** to bring up the **Character Spacing** dialog box.

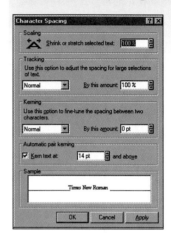

2 Select a Tracking Method

In the **Tracking** section of the dialog box, select a tracking method. The **By this amount** percentage specification changes automatically, but you can change it if you want to fine-tune the tracking.

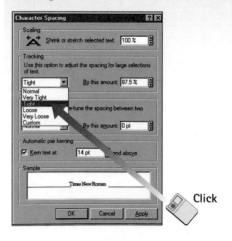

Click

3 Enable Automatic Pair

To automate kerning, make sure the **Automatic pair kerning** section of the dialog box is enabled with a check mark in the box named **Kern text at**. Then specify the size of the font at which automatic kerning is applied. Kerning below 14 points usually doesn't work well.

Click

4 Choose a Kerning Option

If you want to force kerning manually (for type that's smaller than the point at which kerning is automatic), choose a kerning option from the drop-down list. Then check the **Sample** box to see how it looks (usually it doesn't look terrific). You can tweak the kerning by changing the percentage in the **By this amount** box.

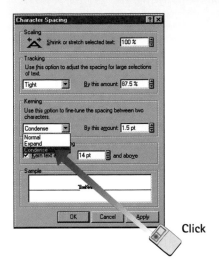

Click

5 Try a Scaling Option

The top of the **Character Spacing** dialog box offers a Scaling option, which doesn't change the spacing, but instead shrinks or expands the characters. Sometimes this works when you have just a bit too much text for a text frame. (However, depending on the font you're using, you may not like the condensed look of the text.)

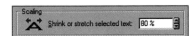

6 Choose Line Spacing

To adjust the leading, select the paragraph(s) you want to change and choose **Format, Line Spacing**.

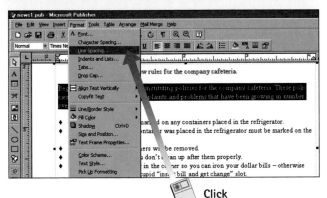

Click

7 Adjust Default on Line Spacing

In the **Line Spacing** dialog box, adjust the default of **1** space in the **Between lines** box. Make the number smaller for tighter copyfitting, or larger to fill an unfilled frame.

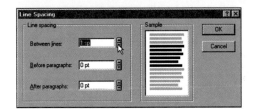

End

How-To Hints

Track and Kern WordArt

You can also track and kern the character spacing in WordArt frames (even though WordArt is really a graphic and not text) with the tools on the **WordArt Formatting** toolbar.

How to Perfect Hyphenation

By default, Publisher automatically hyphenates words in order to make your text look neater. Without hyphenation, words that don't completely fit on a line are pushed to the next line.

You can adjust the way the automatic hyphenation works, and you can also insist on being a part of each hyphenation decision. This is important because there are situations in which hyphenation stops helping and begins harming the look of your text. For instance, consecutive lines that end with hyphens look unprofessional and so does a hyphen at the end of the last line in a text frame (for those stories that are continued in another frame).

Begin

1 Configuring Hyphenation

To configure hyphenation, choose **Tools, Options** from the **menu bar**.

Click

2 Setting the Hyphenation Zone

Move to the **Editing and User Assistance** tab and check the settings in the **Hyphenation** section. You can change the way hyphenation works by changing the **Hyphenation zone** specification. The number indicates how much whitespace must exist in order to force hyphenation. Make the number larger to decrease the number of hyphens. You can also deselect automatic hyphenation by clicking the **Automatically hyphenate in new text frames** option to remove the check mark, but this is not usually a good idea.

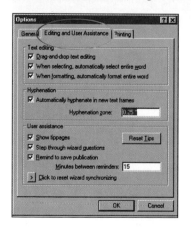

3 Hyphenating Frames

To configure hyphenation for a specific text frame, select the frame and choose **Tools**, **Language**, **Hyphenation** from the **menu bar**. When the **Hyphenation** dialog box appears, change the zone for this story (any connected frames are also changed). If you want to turn off all hyphenation in this story, click the **Automatically hyphenate this story** option to remove the check mark.

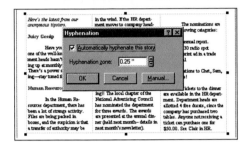

4 Click Manual Hyphenation

Click the **Manual** button in the **Hyphenate** dialog box to approve, change, or eliminate the hyphens that were inserted automatically. Each hyphenated word is displayed with all the possible hyphens. Choose **Yes** to leave the hyphenation as is, or click a different hyphenation point for the word and choose **Yes**. Or, choose **No** if you don't want the word hyphenated. The next hyphenated word is displayed, and this continues throughout the story unless you click the **Close** button.

5 Adding a Hyphenated Phrase

If you have a hyphenated phrase, you can tell Publisher you don't want the hyphen used at the end of a line (which means the words must be kept together on one line, such as Mary-Quite-Contrary). Hold down the **Ctrl+Shift** as you type the hyphens, which tells Publisher these are non-breaking hyphens.

> Stop by the production department to meet the new graphics manager. The gossip editor of this company newsletter thinks it's important to tell everyone that at her previous company the sign on her door read "Mary-Quite-Contrary". Somebody should find the courage to ask the obvious question.

6 Hyphenating a Word

To change the hyphenation for an individual word, select the word and press **Ctrl+Shift+H** to bring up the Hyphenate dialog box. Then click at the alternate hyphenation point and choose **Yes**. If there is no alternate hyphenation point, the **Hyphenate** dialog box offers the options available in Step 4.

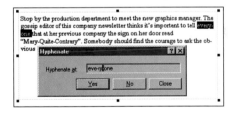

End

How-To Hints

Hyphens in Headlines Are Unprofessional

Never, never permit hyphens in a headline. Widen the text frame, reduce the size of the font, or change the wording—do whatever is necessary to avoid hyphenated headlines.

How to Spell Check Your Publication

There is nothing worse than the embarassment of a mispelled word.

Oops, there is nothing worse than the embarrassment of a misspelled word.

What's worse is that for some reason the fates seem determined to make sure that if you do spell a word wrong, it's a word in a headline—a headline with only a couple of words, printed in a very large font—the sort of thing that makes you wake up in the middle of the night in a cold sweat.

To save you from the agonies of making a fool of yourself, Publisher has a spelling checker. You can configure the spelling checker to show you mistakes as you make them, or wait until you finish your story and then check the spelling.

Begin

1 Select Spell Checking

If you want to check your spelling as you go, choose **Tools**, **Spelling**, **Spelling Options** from the **menu bar**. Then select **Check spelling as you type** and choose **OK**. (If you use a lot of acronyms, especially in technical articles, you might want to tell Publisher to skip words that are uppercase.)

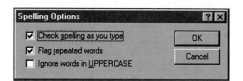

2 Publisher's Misspell Indication

As soon as you press the Spacebar or a punctuation character to indicate the end of the word, Publisher underlines any word not in its dictionary (which probably means you misspelled it). Sometimes, instead of underlining, it automatically corrects the spelling. In this case, I typed "somtimes," which was automatically changes to "sometimes."

> The FAT32 file system available for Windows 95 and Windows 98 has both advantages and disadvanteges. Sometimes, |

3 Right-Click to Correct

Right-click any word that has a red squiggly line beneath it to see a list of suggested replacements. Choose the correct word. If no accurate suggestions are available, choose **Check Spelling** for more options (which is covered in the next steps).

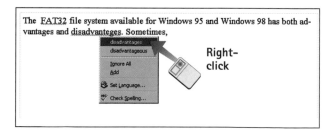

4 Spell Check at End of Story

If you didn't select the "check as you go" option (you prefer not to be annoyed by the squiggly lines and want to wait until you've finished your publication), you can check a story by selecting its first frame and pressing **F7**. The spelling checker stops at the first word that isn't in the Publisher dictionary.

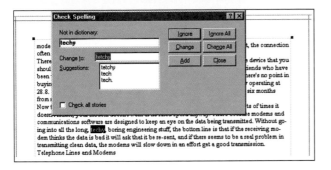

5 Choose Ignore

If the word is just fine (although not in the Publisher dictionary), choose **Ignore** to let your word remain this time, or choose **Ignore All** to let your word remain as is throughout the document.

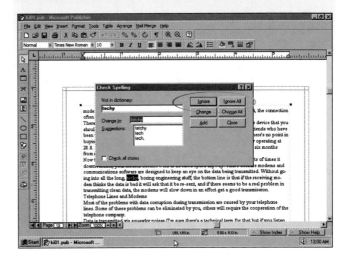

6 Choose Change

To accept Publisher's suggestion, highlight the correct suggested word and choose **Change**. To accept the same change throughout the story, choose **Change All**.

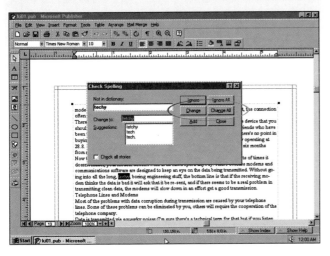

7 Choose Add

If your word is fine and you expect to use it in other stories, choose **Add** to put your word in the Dictionary. This means that the spelling checker won't stop on that word again.

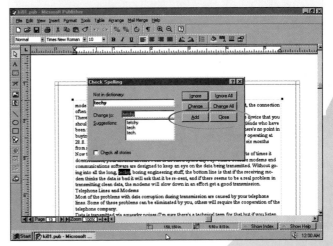

Continues

8 Spell Check Multiple Frames

The spelling checker continues through your story, over multiple frames, until it reaches the end of the story. (You can stop the spell check at any time by choosing **Close**.) It then offers to check the rest of your publication—it's a good idea to accept the offer by clicking **Yes**.

9 Click OK

When the spelling checker finishes its work, it announces the fact. Click **OK**.

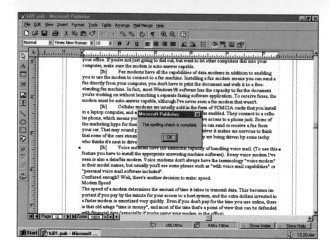

10 Skipping Spell Check

If you create a paragraph or a story that is replete with technical terms, proper names, or even deliberate misspellings, you can skip the spell check. Select the text and choose **Tools**, **Language**, **Set Language** from the **menu bar**.

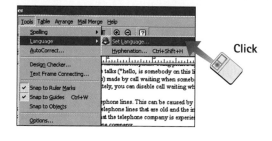

Click

11 Choose No Proofing

In the **Language** dialog box, scroll to the top of the list to find **(no proofing)**. Select it and choose **OK**.

12 Adding Your Own Words

Publisher has a list of commonly misspelled words (remember how it corrected "sometimes" automatically) and their correct spellings; it uses the list to AutoCorrect your spelling. You can add your own frequently misspelled words to the list by choosing **Tools**, **AutoCorrect** from the **menu bar**. When the **AutoCorrect** dialog box opens, enter the wrong and right spelling, and then choose **Add**.

13 Adding Your Own Phrases

You can also use AutoCorrect to substitute frequently used phrases for a code you type (be sure that the code you enter in the **Replace** box isn't a real word). As soon as you press the Spacebar or a punctuation character, your code disappears and the phrase appears.

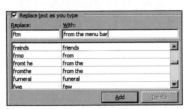

End

How-To Hints

Check Your Web Publication Elements

If you're publishing to the Web, the spelling checker can check the text you place on buttons or the text you use for labels. Information about preparing publications for the Web is found in Chapter 6, "Creating a Web Publication."

Check Your Own WordArt

You're not totally safe from errors—the spelling checker can only check text (text frames and tables). You're on your own with your WordArt frames.

Repeated Words Are Fixed, Too

The spelling checker is configured, by default, to catch repeated words such as "put the the pen on the table." This is very handy.

How to Check the Design

Your publication's design is almost as important as the messages within it. Unfortunately, a layout mistake can make the idea of reading a story less attractive. There are all sorts of research studies that indicate that if it's hard to follow text, the average reader doesn't bother to read it. Too much eye movement is annoying (don't put a graphic in the middle of a text column), too many things to look at on a page is exasperating (don't fill the page with numerous small text frames).

Publisher has a feature that looks at your publication's overall design and makes suggestions to improve it. It's like having a publishing consultant stop in and give you a no-charge opinion. How nifty!

Begin

1 Choose Design Checker

To check your design, choose **Tools**, **Design Checker** from the **menu bar**.

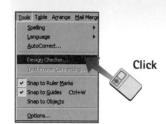

Click

2 Select Pages to Be Reviewed

In the **Design Checker** dialog box, specify whether you want to check **All** or specific **Pages**. (If you have a background design, you should check it out, too.)

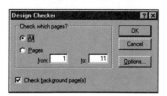

3 Design Checker Dialog Box

The design checker starts with the background and then moves through your pages. When a problem is perceived, a dialog box notifies you. Notice that the frame involved in the problem is selected for you by the Design Checker so you can work on the problem if you want.

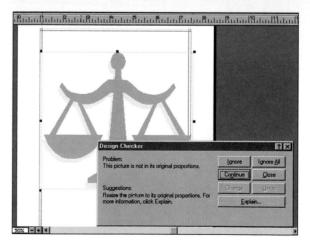

4 Ignore or Fix Problems

Choose **Ignore** if you want to leave the design the way it is, or **Ignore All** if you want all instances of this type of design problem ignored. Otherwise, you must fix the problem. Choose **Continue** to move on. (If you try to choose **Continue** without fixing or ignoring the problem, the Design Checker stubbornly refuses to move on.)

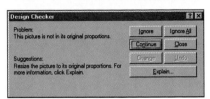

5 Click OK

When everything is fixed (or ignored), the Design Checker tells you it has completed its job. Click **OK**.

6 Choose Options

You can control the design elements that are checked by choosing **Options** on the initial **Design Checker** dialog box. Click any problem you know you don't care about to deselect it.

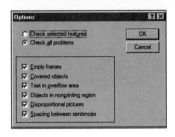

End

How-To Hints

Use Your Judgment

Many of the Design Checker's suggestions are really a matter of taste, and you should feel free to ignore those items that you created for a deliberate reason. The design problem you can't ignore is text in an overflow area. You must copyfit the text to fit or create another frame and continue the text.

Changed Graphics Are Okay

The most common fault the Design Checker finds is that graphic images are not in their original proportion (you've stretched or shrunken a clip art image). If the image isn't distorted, feel free to ignore this warning.

How to Work with Bindings

Any publication that requires more than one piece of paper should be bound. Don't panic, binding just means "attached."

Most of the time, a bound publication is printed on two sides, resulting in a *verso* (left) page for the even numbered pages, and a *recto* (right) page for the odd numbered pages. However, you can print and bind a publication that's designed to print only on one side of the paper. (I use this method for training books in order to leave a blank left page for students to take notes.)

No matter which binding method you use, you have to design your publication around it. The binding might cover text or graphics otherwise. The left page needs binding space (called a *gutter*) on the right side and the right page has its gutter on the left side.

Begin

1 Choose Layout Guides

To force empty space for binding, choose **Arrange**, **Layout Guides** from the **menu bar**.

2 Change the Inside Margin

If you're printing on both sides of the paper, be sure the **Create Two Backgrounds With Mirrored Guides** option is selected on the **Layout Guides** dialog box. Change the size of the **Inside** margin to match the gutter size you need (which depends on your binding method).

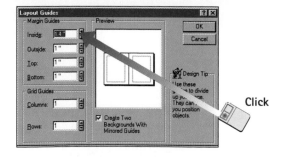

Click

3 Increase the Left Margin

If you're printing only on one side of the paper (you might want to leave a blank page on one side of the publication for readers to use for notes), increase the margin for the side of the paper that will be bound. It's most common to have the printed page on the right side of the publication, so adjust the left margin.

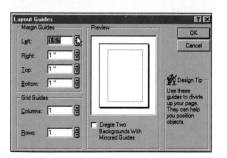

4 Change the Background

If you're using the background for page numbers or titles, design the gutter for the background page. If you've already designed the background, you probably need to adjust the graphic to match the new margin. For more information about using the background, see "How to Create Background Elements" in Chapter 4, "Adding Special Elements."

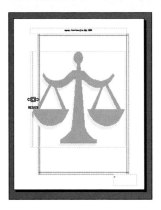

5 Using Rulers

To make sure the foreground pages don't print on top of the background text, use ruler guides to give yourself margins. Use the ruler guide on the gutter side when you're working on the page. (The gutter side changes as you work on odd or even pages.) See "How to Use Ruler Guides" in Chapter 1, "Getting Started."

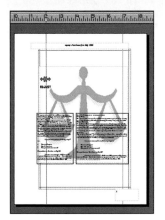

End

How-To Hints

How to Staple the Middle of Newsletters

If you produce newsletters, you can fold the paper and then push staples into the fold. You'll need a long stapler, which is available at most office supply stores.

Set the Binding Margins First

If your publication has columns (like a newspaper or a newsletter), remember that the columns grow thinner as you expand the gutter. If you wait until you've finished your publication to set these binding margins, you may find that some text overflows the frames. That's why you should set your binding margins before you begin work on the publication.

How-To Hints

Some Options for Binding Your Publication

There are lots of ways to bind a publication, from pushing in staples to attaching professionally glued covers. For a thick publication or a fancy cover, you'll probably want to contact a professional printing service or a bindery.

How to Work with Crop and Registration Marks

Crop marks are special markings that must be printed (outside the margins of the publication) when the paper and your publication are not the same size. They provide the guide lines for cutting the paper.

Registration marks are also printed outside the margins of the publication, and they indicate the place at which the pages line up as they pass through the printer. This device is used by outside printing companies for printing in multiple passes. The printing company needs a separate printed page for each color in your publication.

Begin

1 Choose Print

Crop marks are inserted automatically during the printing process. To print the crop marks for your publication, choose **File**, **Print** from the **menu bar** (or press **Ctrl+P**).

Click

3 Notice Crop Marks

The printed copy displays the crop marks needed to cut the paper accurately.

2 Select Print Crop Marks

In the **Print** dialog box, make sure that the **Print Crop Marks** option is selected.

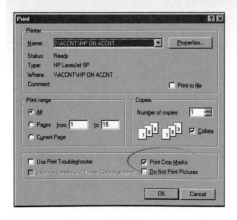

4 Select Show All Printer Marks

When you set up your publication for outside printing, be sure to select the **Show all printer marks** option. (The option is offered in the third step of the setup.) All the information you need about printing to an outside printing service is found in Chapter 8, "Printing Your Publication."

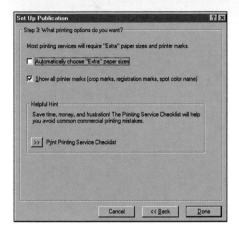

5 Notice Registration Marks

When you print a proof copy (and when the printer prints the publication), the registration marks are printed along with the crop marks.

6 Line Up Registration Marks

Notice that the registration mark provides a way to make very precise connections. The lines and the circles must both line up on at least two registration marks to assure crisp printing.

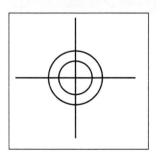

End

Project

Project 2

Here's a follow-along exercise for creating a publication, using the skills covered in Chapter 1, "Getting Started," through Chapter 5, "Tweaking Your Publication."

We'll move along a little faster than usual in this exercise because there are a lot of functions and features to use; some of the steps will take for granted that you've read and learned the basic stuff.

No wizard—this time you build your own publication. It's a notice for a lawn sale. It has to look slick and professional because all the neighbors who are participating want to get good prices as you clean out your attics, basements, and garages. If the image is right, the prices will follow.

1 Get a Blank Page

When Publisher opens to the Catalog, choose **Exit Catalog** to get to a blank page.

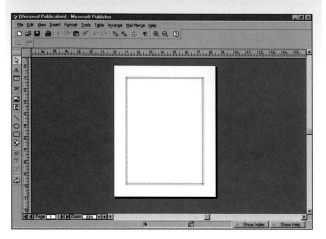

2 Create a Frame

Click the **Text Frame** tool on the **Objects** toolbar and drag a text frame across the top of the page. This will be a headline.

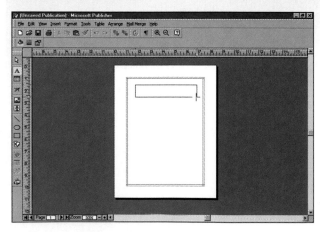

3 Enter a Headline

Press **F9** to zoom in so you can see what you're typing. Enter a headline for this flyer.

Not Just Junque

4 Pick a Font

Select the text by dragging your mouse across it, and then click the arrow next to the **font** box on the **Formatting** toolbar to select a new font (pick a font with personality). Click the arrow next to the **font size** box and choose a larger font size.

5 Center the Headline

Press **F9** to zoom back out. You can see that the headline needs to be centered, so click the **Center** button on the **Formatting** toolbar.

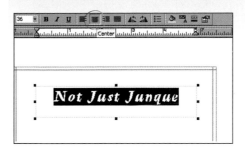

6 Choose More Styles

To make the headline even more attention getting, click the **Line/Border Style** button on the **Formatting** toolbar and choose **More Styles** from the **drop-down menu**.

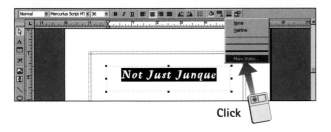

Click

7 Select a Border

Click the **BorderArt** tab when the **Border Style** dialog box opens, and then scroll through the patterns to find just the right border. Select it, click the **arrow** next to the **Color** box, and pick a color for the border. Choose **OK** to put the border on the text frame.

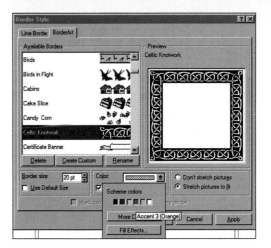

Continues

8 Enlarge the Frame

Select the text frame and drag a resize handle to enlarge the text frame so that both the border and the text are showing. (If you choose a thinner border, you won't need to take this step, but sometimes a thick border is what's needed for the right effect.)

9 Open Design Gallery

To add an arresting design element to the flyer, click the **Design Gallery Object** button on the **Objects** toolbar.

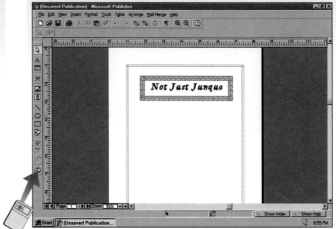

Click

10 Choose Attention Getters

When the Design Gallery opens, choose **Attention Getters** in the left pane, and then choose a design in the right pane. Click **Insert Object**.

11 Position the Object

Move and resize the object to position it the way you like it.

12 Enter Your Text

Click the text frame inside the object and replace the placeholder text with your own words. This text frame is configured for automatic copyfitting, so if you enter more characters than the original text had, your font gets smaller to accommodate the size of the frame.

13 Choose a Fill Color

Click the background design (behind the text frame) and then click the **Fill Color** button on the **Formatting** toolbar. Choose a color that matches the border color you used (or, at the least, a color that doesn't clash).

14 Type in the Information

Create another text frame and fill in the information about the sale. Use the tools on the **Formatting** toolbar to enhance the placement and look of the text.

15 Add Symbols or Arrows

For extra pizzazz, add symbols or arrows (or both). Click where you want to have a special character and then choose **Insert**, **Symbol** from the **menu bar**.

Continues

16 Choose a Symbol

When the **Symbol** dialog box opens, scroll through the characters to find something you think will work. (You can change fonts to search other character sets.) Click a symbol that has possibilities and hold the left mouse button down to see it enlarged in order to decide whether it's the symbol you want to use.

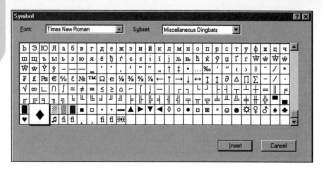

17 Insert the Symbol

Choose **Insert** to place the symbol where you clicked before you opened the **Symbol** dialog box. Repeat if you want to add other symbols.

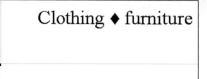

18 Check Your Spelling

Check your spelling to avoid embarrassment. Click the first text frame and press **F7** to begin a spell check. In this case, of course, the spell checker found an error. Choose **Ignore All** to tell the spell checker that this word should be ignored no matter how many times it appears in this publication.

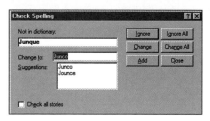

19 Make Spelling Corrections

When the spell checker on the first frame is completed, Publisher offers to check all the other text frames in the publication. Choose **Yes**. Make any corrections you need to.

20 Check Your Design

To check the overall design, choose **Tools**, **Design Checker** from the **menu bar**. When the first **Design Checker** dialog box displays, select **All** (to determine the number of pages to check; in this case there's only one page anyway) and click **OK**.

21 Correct Any Problems

If the design checker finds a problem, it selects the appropriate frame. Work on the frame to correct the problem. Choose **Continue**.

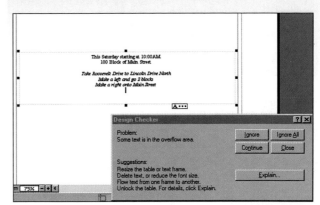

22 Save Your Publication

Click the **Save** icon on the **Standard** toolbar and when the **Save As** dialog box opens, name your publication and choose **Save**. Print a lot of copies and hang them up in stores and on telephone poles.

End

Task

6

Creating a Web Publication

*I*t doesn't matter how big your mailing list is or how many copies of your publication you think you can give away: You'll never reach as many potential readers as you can if you publish your masterpiece on the World Wide Web.

Of course, you don't have to chop down forests to provide enough paper for all those readers; one copy of your publication is all you need to reach an unlimited number of readers.

However, you can't just deliver a printed publication to a Web site and ask to be displayed. There are programming rules, programming codes, and graphic conversion programs that have to be followed. It's all terribly complicated—unless you use Publisher.

In this chapter you learn how easy it is to tell Publisher what you want in your Web publication. Publisher does all that techy stuff for you, behind the scenes. You can use these handy tools to create a Web page from scratch or to convert your favorite publications to Web pages. ●

How to Set Up a Web Publication

Even if you're not in charge of your company's Web site, as you become adept in Publisher you'll be producing such great graphical publications that somebody will eventually say "We need that on the Web site."

Creating publications for the Web requires some special steps and distinctive design approaches, but don't worry, Publisher is equipped to provide an incredible amount of assistance.

Begin

1 Choose the Web Site Wizard

Choose **Web Sites** in the Catalog's **Publications by Wizard** tab.

2 Select a Design

In the right pane, scroll through the available Web page design layouts and select the one you like; then choose **Start Wizard**.

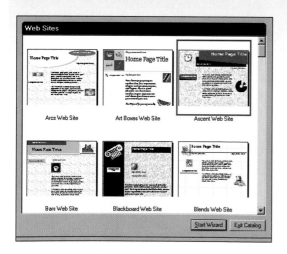

3 Provide Information for the Wizard

Select **Next** in the **Web Site Wizard** pane and choose your preferences, continuing to click **Next** as you complete each page; then choose **Finish** and hide the wizard.

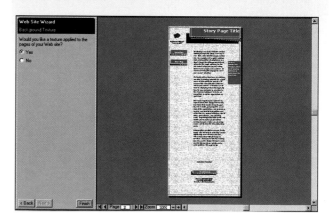

4 Enter Text

Select the text frames in the Web page and substitute your own words for the placeholder text.

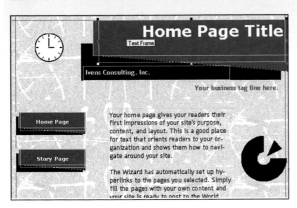

5 Replace the Art Work

Double-click any graphic to replace it with artwork that's more suitable for your message.

6 Use a Blank Web Page

If you want to build your Web page from scratch, use the Catalog's **Blank Publications** tab and select **Web Page**. Choose **Create** to begin building your Web publication. Create text and graphic frames as you need them. (The Catalog appears automatically when you first start Publisher, but if you're already working in the software, choose **File**, **New** from the **menu bar** to open the Catalog.)

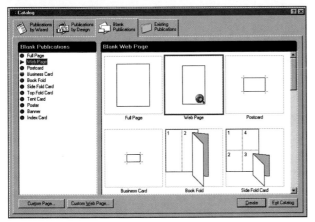

End

How-To Hints

Use the Wizard Until You're Comfortable

You can choose either a predesigned page (with a wizard) or a blank page (and add each element yourself) for your Web publication. It's probably a good idea to use the wizard for your first experiment in Web pages.

How to Create Navigation Bars

Navigation bars are those parts of a Web page that you use to move to other parts of the Web site.

A true navigation bar is called a *vertical navigation bar*. You can also insert a *horizontal navigation bar*, which is really a text frame with text that is configured as a hyperlink. (If you use the Web Page Wizard, you're offered the choice of a vertical or horizontal navigation bar, or you can choose both.) See the next pages for information about creating the actual hyperlinks.

You can create your own navigation bar or edit the one placed there by the wizard.

Begin

1 Select the Wizard-Inserted Navigation Bar

If you used the Web Page Wizard for your publication, click the vertical navigation bar that was inserted automatically. When it's selected, a wizard button appears on the bottom of the frame; you can click it to change the bar's color and design scheme.

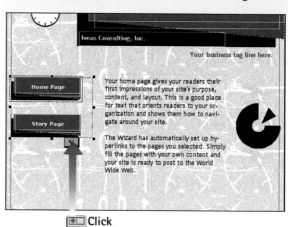

Click

2 Create Your Own Navigation Bar

To create a navigation bar, click the **Design Gallery Object** tool on the **Objects** toolbar.

3 Choose a Navigation Bar Design

When the Design Gallery opens, choose **Web Navigation Bars** as the category, and then choose the design you want to use for your main (vertical) bar from the offerings in the right pane. Choose **Insert Object** to put the bar on your page.

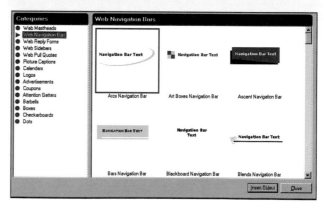

4 Position the Navigation Bar

When the navigation bar is on your page, move it to an appropriate spot on your page. Usually, it's best to put the bar in the page's upper-left section—Web users have learned to look there for navigation bars.

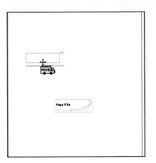

5 Insert the Text for the Navigation Bar

Select the placeholder text on the navigation bar elements and replace it with something more specific (and more creative). For example, if you're linking to a story about the UFO you saw the last time you took a walk in the swamp, call it My UFO Sighting.

6 Format the Text

Even though you're creating a Web publication, this is still a text frame and you can use all the text formatting tools available. For example, you can change the font, make the text bold, or fill the frame with a color.

End

How-To Hints

Navigation Bars Are Easier for Your Audience

You can use a single word or a short phrase within a regular text frame as a hyperlink, but if you have a lot of links, it's a good idea to provide a navigation bar in one section of your home page.

How to Add Hyperlinks

When your publication is on the Web, readers can't go through the exercise of moistening a finger and turning the page. You have to give them a device to get to the next page. That device is a *hyperlink*, and you can add a hyperlink to text or a graphic object.

Begin

1 Select Text

To add a hyperlink to text, select the word(s) for the hyperlink.

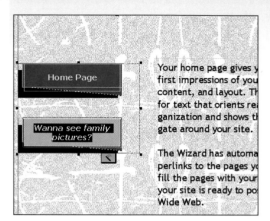

2 Choose the Hyperlink Command

Right-click the selected text and choose **Hyperlink** from the **shortcut menu** (or press **Ctrl+K** for a keyboard shortcut).

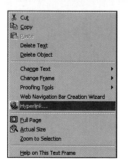

3 Select the Hyperlink Options

In the **Hyperlink** dialog box, select the options you need to link your text and its target. Choose **OK**.

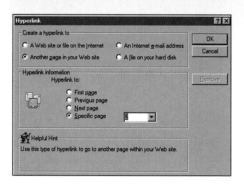

4 Hyperlinked Text Is Underlined

When you return to your text frame, the text you selected for the hyperlink is underlined.

5 Use a Graphic

To add a hyperlink to a graphic image, right-click anywhere in the graphic frame and choose **Hyperlink**; then specify the options you need in the **Hyperlink** dialog box.

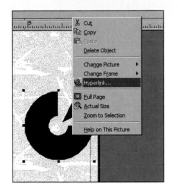

6 Check the Graphic Link

When you choose **OK** to close the **Hyperlink** dialog box, check the graphic (it's not underlined the way text is) by placing your mouse pointer anywhere on the frame. You should see a ScreenTip that displays the link.

End

How-To Hints

Hyperlinks Can Do Lots of Things

Hyperlinks don't have to move readers to another page in your Web site; you can use them to link to another Web site or to a file you've made accessible.

How to Add Hot Spots

A *hot spot* is a place on an object that holds a hyperlink. You can have numerous hot spots on one object.

If you've played with any children's story CD-ROMs, you've probably clicked specific parts of a picture to launch another story—click the cow and see a cow story, click the tree and see birds flying. Those are examples of hot spots.

Begin

1 Click the Hot Spot Tool

Click the **Hot Spot Tool** button on the **Objects** toolbar.

Click

2 Draw the Hot Spot

Position your pointer where the upper-left corner of the hot spot belongs and drag down and to the right to create a hot spot. In this case, the hot spot is being positioned around the baby's head.

3 Configure the Hyperlink

The **Hyperlink** dialog box opens automatically when you release the mouse button. Select the options you need for this hyperlink and choose **OK**.

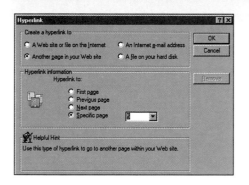

4 Check the Hyperlink

Position your pointer over the hot spot to check the hyperlink displayed in the ScreenTip.

5 Create a Hot Spot with a Shape

Another way to add a hot spot to a picture is to add an element you can use for the hot spot such as a shape. (This is not technically a hot spot but it works the same way.) Click a **Shape tool** on the **Objects** toolbar and add it to the picture. Then place a hot spot on the shape, following the steps described earlier.

6 Create Multiple Hot Spots

You can repeat the processes explained here to create multiple hot spots. While you work in Publisher you'll see the frame for each hot spot on your page. (The frames aren't displayed when your publication is on the Web, but your reader's pointer changes to a **hand** to indicate a link.)

End

How-To Hints

Don't Use Hot Spots Where They Aren't Needed

Don't use hot spots on standard Web navigation objects such as **Next** or **Previous** buttons. The entire object should be the hot spot in these cases.

5

How to Add Pages to a Web Publication

Whether you use a wizard-designed publication or create your own from scratch, you probably will add pages to your Web masterpiece as additional information needs to be disseminated.

Begin

1 Use the Insert Command

Choose **Insert**, **Page** from the **menu bar**.

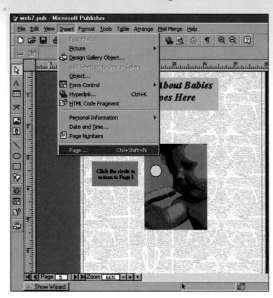

2 Choose a Page Type

The **Insert Page** dialog box for Web pages offers choices specifically for Web publications. Start by clicking the arrow next to the **Available page types** box and picking the type of page you need. If you want this page listed on your navigation bar, make sure that option is selected at the bottom of the dialog box.

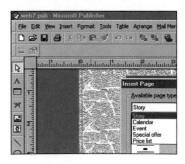

3 Specify Other Options

Choose **More Options** on the **Insert Page** dialog box to see additional choices for inserting this new page. Choose **OK** twice to insert the page into your publication.

4 Put a Title on the Page

It's always a good idea to add a title to every page. Unlike printed publications, Web documents aren't treated as a continuous story, and each page exists for specific information. Don't forget to format the text and frame; plain text is dull on the Web.

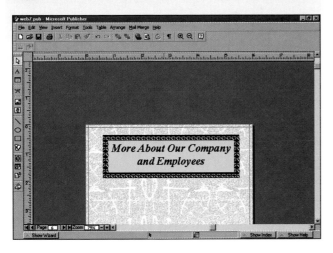

5 Locate the Navigation Bar Link

Move to your navigation bar (which should be on your first page, which is called your home page) and locate the hyperlink to your new page. Hold your pointer over the navigation bar objects to see the ScreenTips.

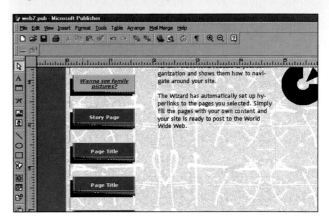

6 Give the Navigation Object a Title

Select and then change the placeholder text in the navigation bar object to indicate the subject matter on the new page. You can either repeat the page title or enter a catchy phrase that lures people to the page.

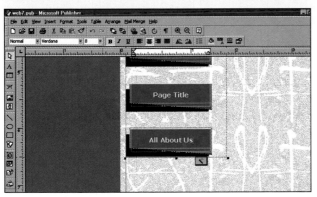

End

How-To Hints

Put Everything on the Navigation Bar

Although Publisher 98 offers an option for listing a new page on the navigation bar, don't think of it as optional. Always select this link so your readers can navigate easily through all your publication's pages.

Adding Sounds and Animation to Web Pages

Some of the fun of visiting Web sites is hearing music or sound effects and watching stuff prance around the screen in a frenzy of animation. You can provide those elements for your Web visitors, too.

Background sound is music (or noise, if you prefer) you attach to a Web page, and it becomes an element for the page, not for a particular object.

2 Specify a Sound File

In the **Web Properties** dialog box, move to the **Page** tab. In the dialog box's **Background sound** section, enter the name of the sound file you want to use in the **File name** box. Click the **Browse** button to locate the sound file if you don't have the folder and filename memorized. Choose to *loop* (replay) the sound file incessantly while the reader is viewing this page, or choose to have it play a specific number of times. Click **OK**. (Nothing happens—you won't hear the sound in Publisher, only when you're viewing the page in a browser.)

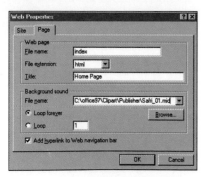

Begin

1 Opening the Web Properties

To add sound that's attached to the Web page (it starts when the Web page opens in a browser), you need to configure the properties for the Web page. With your Web page in the Publisher window, choose **File**, **Web Properties** from the **menu bar**.

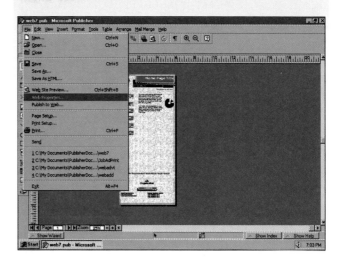

3 Create a Picture Frame

Click the **Clip Gallery Tool** button on the **Objects** toolbar and drag your mouse to create a frame on your Web page.

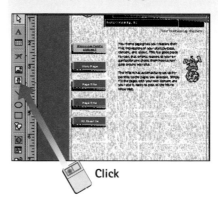

Click

4 Choose the Picture File

The Clip Gallery opens automatically when you release the mouse. Move to the **Motion Clips** tab. Double-click to select a picture and insert it in the frame.

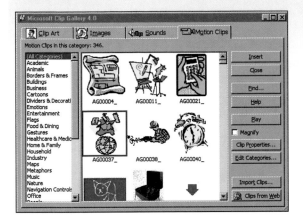

5 Position the Picture Frame

Move the picture frame so that it isn't on any part of a text frame. (That prevents the animation on the Web and you'll have a static picture.) If necessary, resize it.

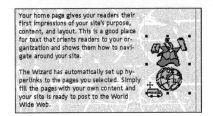

6 Preview the Publication on the Web

Because neither the sound nor the animation works in Publisher, choose **File**, **Web Site Preview** from the **menu bar**. When your browser opens, you hear your sounds and see your animation.

End

How-To Hints

Sound Files Can Be Very Large

Some sound files are quite large and if your page is filled with lots of elements and graphics, adding sound may make the process of loading it into the **browser** window slow enough to annoy your reader. Preview the page for friends and coworkers and see what they think.

How to Check the Web Design

There are a number of design issues you have to think about when you publish for the Web. Do you have all the correct elements to make your hyperlinks work properly? Are your text and graphic frames placed for easy reading? (Web readers don't expect to see page after page of text-based articles.)

Worry not! Publisher 98 has a built-in design checker that goes over your publication with a critical attitude. This nit-picking expert should be consulted before you begin thinking about publishing to the Web.

Begin

1 Open the Design Checker

Choose **Tools**, **Design Checker** from the menu bar.

2 Select the Pages to Check

When the **Design Checker** dialog box opens, you can either choose **All** to check the entire publication or select **Pages** and specify a range (including a begin and end page number that's the same if you have only a page you think you should check).

3 Set the Terms

Choose **Options** on the **Design Checker** dialog box to specify what you want the design checker to cover. Choose **Check selected features** and then click the appropriate check boxes to deselect the items you don't care about. Click **OK** to return to the **Design Checker** dialog box, and then click **OK** again to start the check.

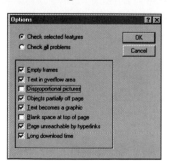

4 Read the Problem Dialog Box

The check stops at each problem and offers choices for solving the problem. Choose **Ignore** to ignore this problem; choose **Ignore All** to ignore all problems like the one presented; choose the solution button. (In this case the solution that's offered is **Change**, while an empty frame problem has a solution button that says **Delete Frame**.)

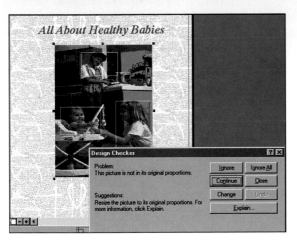

5 Continue the Checkup

After you fix the problem, choose **Continue** to move on to the next problem.

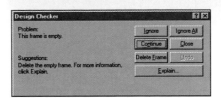

7 Finish the Checkup

When the design checker is finished, it announces that fact. Click **OK** to tell it to go away.

End

6 Check Your Speed

When a reader opens your publication, the process involved is really a download (from your Web site to the reader's screen). Publisher offers to check the download speed. It reports back that it's worried if it finds large, complicated graphics and suggests you change them. Choose **Yes** to look for problems; click **No** if you don't care about this issue.

How-To Hints

Hints to Use the Design Checker

The **Continue** button in the design checker doesn't work until you've fixed the problem. The checker moves on automatically if you opt to ignore the problem.

- Choose **Close** to stop the design checker at any time.

- Choose **Explain** to open a **Help** page that explains what's wrong and how to fix it. (You may have to drag the **Design Checker** dialog box over in order to see the bottom of the **Help** page.)

TASK 8

How to Preview Your Web Publication

Don't send your publication to your Web site without making sure it looks the way you think it will. Working in the **Publisher** window does not provide a real look at a Web publication—you need to test the way things work as well as the way everything looks.

Begin

1 Open the Preview Program

Choose **File, Web Site Preview** from the **menu bar**. If you only want to preview one page, move to that page before selecting this command.

2 Choose the Pages to Preview

When the **Web Site Preview** dialog box opens, it offers a choice of previewing the **Web site** (all the pages in your publication) or the **Current page**. Make your choice and choose **OK**.

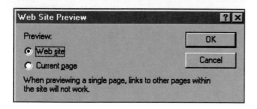

3 Publisher Converts Your Publication

Publisher prepares your publication for the Web. Depending on your machine's speed and your publication's complexity, this could take a couple of seconds or a minute-plus.

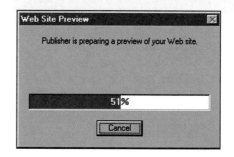

4 Examine the Browser Window

Your default browser opens with your publication in the window. The first thing to check is any object you placed a hyperlink in; it is this way you make sure your pointer turns into a hand when it is on the object.

5 Test the Hyperlinks

Click each hyperlink object to make sure you jump to the right place. In this case, the hyperlink moved me to the right page, and I notice that the heading that seemed centered in my **Publisher** window is off center in the **browser** window.

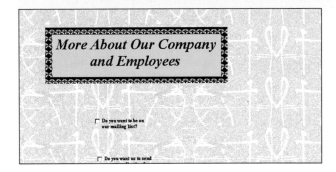

6 Close the Browser

Close the **browser** window (click the **X** in the upper-right corner) and you're returned to the **Publisher** window. Now you can fix any problems you found.

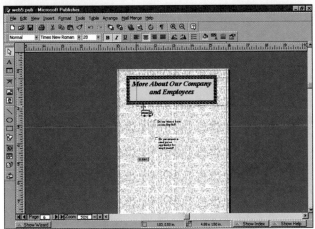

End

How-To Hints

You Can Check One Page at a Time

You can choose to preview a single page, which is helpful if you want to take a fast check of a page you think might have problems. However, a single-page Web preview does not activate your hyperlinks, so you won't be able to see if they work.

How to Convert Publications to Web Pages

If you've created a really terrific publication, it might be suitable for your Web site. You don't have to reconstruct it as a Web publication—you can convert it.

Begin

1 Open the Conversion Program

Choose **File, Create Web Site from Current Publication** from the **menu bar**.

2 Check the Design

The design checker steps right up and offers to check the design before the conversion is complete. Say **Yes** and tell the checker to check **All pages**. Deal with each problem as it is presented. For more information about using the design checker, see Task 6, "How to Check the Design," in Chapter 5.

3 Insert Hyperlinks if Needed

If the design checker tells you that a page cannot be reached, you must create a hyperlink to it. This is always a problem if your publication has more than one page, and it's a good idea to choose **Close** to stop the design checker to take care of this detail.

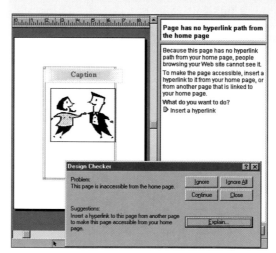

4 Create Links to All Pages

It's easiest to create a navigation bar from the Design Gallery, although you could create individual hyperlink objects for each page of your publication. For details about inserting a navigation bar, see Task 2, "How to Create Navigation Bars," in Chapter 6. Start the design checker again and solve any remaining problems.

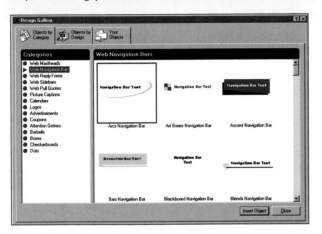

5 Preview the Publication on the Web

After you've fixed any problems, choose **File, Web Site Preview** from the **menu bar**. Tell Publisher you want to preview the entire publication by choosing **Web site** in the **Web Site Preview** dialog box.

6 Check Everything in Your Browser Window

When your browser opens, check your publication carefully. If you think it will look just fine to the people who visit your site, you've just saved yourself all the work of creating it again. Save your publication with a new filename.

Caption

How-To Hints

A Converted Document Is a New Document

When you choose the command to convert a publication to a Web publication, you're really creating a new document. You have to save it again with a new filename.

Conversion Isn't Always the Answer

Conversion doesn't always work well because many elements that are created for printed publications don't translate properly to a Web page (especially lots of text), but it's always worth trying. If the end result looks so yechy you're embarrassed when it displays in your browser window, you'll just have to redo it as a Web publication.

End

How to Publish Your Publication to the Web

It's not the norm for all the Publisher experts (as you're becoming) to be in charge of a company Web site. Companies usually have *Webmasters* who control the site; you may have to print your publication to a file and let the Webmaster fetch and transfer it to the Web site. If your company runs an *intranet* (residing on a network server), you might be able to arrange to publish directly to that site. As a result, it's far more common to save your publication as a file and store it in a folder, where it can be moved to the Web site.

Special software, which is discussed here, is required if you are the person in your company who publishes directly to the Web site.

2 Saving to Your Hard Drive

When the **Save as HTML** dialog box opens, you'll see that Publisher has created a folder named **Publish** under the folder that contains your Publisher documents. (If it didn't, choose **New Folder** and create it yourself.) Click **OK** to save your publication as a Web publication in that folder.

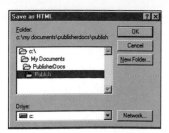

Begin

1 Publishing to a File

You can save your publication to a folder either on your network server or on your own hard drive. To accomplish this, choose **File**, **Save As HTML** from the **menu bar**.

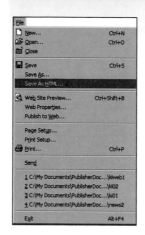

3 Saving to the Network

If you have a company intranet or a special folder your Webmaster uses, click the **Network** button on the **Save as HTML** dialog box. The **Map Network Drive** dialog box opens with the server highlighted and the next available drive letter in the **Drive** box. Save your file in the place designated by your company.

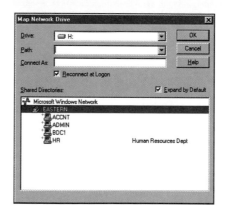

4 Install the Web Publishing Wizard

You need the Microsoft Web Publishing Wizard in order to publish to a Web site. When you installed Publisher, a shortcut for the wizard setup was installed on your desktop. Close Publisher and double-click the shortcut to install the software. Restart your computer.

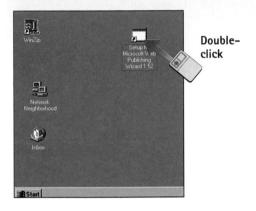

Double-click

5 Run the Publishing Wizard

After the wizard is installed, you can use the **Publish to Web** command, which appears on the **File** menu. Of course, you must open the publication first. Follow the wizard's instructions as you fill out the information your ISP requires.

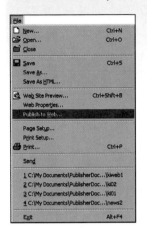

6 Run the Wizard as a Separate Program

You don't have to be working in Publisher to deliver your publication to your Web site. After you complete the installation and restart your computer, your **Start** menu has a listing for the software.

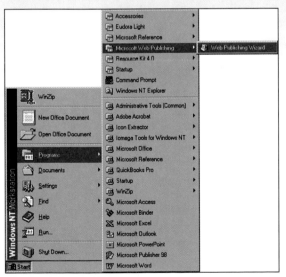

How-To Hints

Check the Rules First

You must contact your ISP (Internet service provider) for instructions in order to publish directly to your Web site. Each ISP has specific requirements for publications.

End

Task

7

Creating Specialty Publications

Your list of things to do includes ordering stationery for the company, sending a greeting card to a friend who should be congratulated for passing the bar exam, and finding something relaxing to do during your lunch hour.

Publisher can take care of everything. There are a host of specialty publications available in Publisher (done with the help of some very clever wizards). You can design matching stationery (everything from business cards to the expense report forms you have to fill in to get those parking fees back). You can create greeting cards. You can make wonderful paper airplanes, complete with instructions on how to fold and fly them.

In this chapter you have fun working with some of the Publisher publications that provide relief from the usual daily grind. ●

How to Create Greeting Cards

The price of greeting cards has risen faster and higher than the price of gasoline. (I'm giving away my age.) If you enjoy sending cards to friends and family for all sorts of occasions, you're parting with more than spare change.

Publisher can help you produce your own cards, which means you'll save money. More important (and more fun), your cards will be original and personal.

Most greeting cards have four pages (one is usually blank), even though you only need one piece of paper.

Begin

1 Choose Greeting Cards

Bring up the Catalog by choosing **File**, **New** from the **menu bar**. (If you just launched Publisher, the Catalog appears automatically.) Click the **Greeting Cards** entry on the **Publications by Wizard** tab to expand it.

2 Choose Specific Card

Choose the specific type of card you need from the expanded list, and then select a style from the right pane. Click **Start Wizard** to begin.

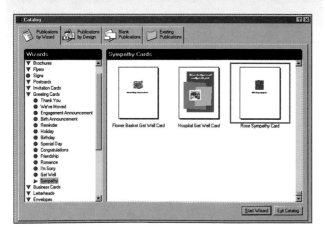

3 Select a Layout

When the **wizard** pane opens, click **Next** to begin making decisions. The first determination is the layout. As you select a layout, the card changes so you can see the results. When you find one you like, click **Next**.

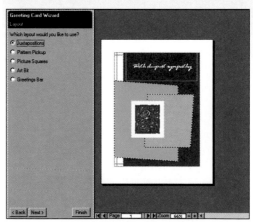

4 Add a Sentiment

Continue to give the wizard your configuration options (paper size, folding scheme, and color scheme). The wizard asks if you want to see some verses. Click **Browse** to see the sentiments available. If you see anything you like, select it and choose **OK** (you can change it later). If you want to write original sentiments, choose **Cancel**.

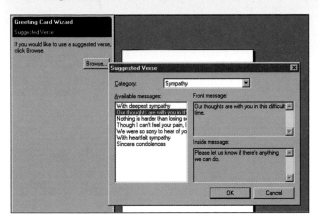

5 Choose Finish

Choose **Finish** in the **wizard** pane and then click **Hide Wizard** so you can work on your card.

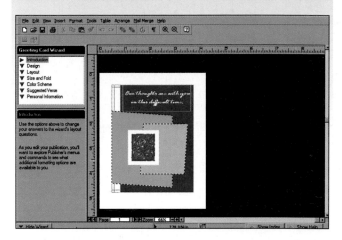

6 Touch Up the Card

Create new text or replace graphics (some are on the background).

I'm so sorry to hear your computer crashed. I hope you remembered to do nightly backups.

How-To Hints

Choosing a Filename

After you've created a greeting card, save the file with a name that indicates the recipient. I know someone who sent the same card to the same person a couple of times. Very embarrassing!

7 Choose Print

Choose **File**, **Print** to print your card; notice that it's ready for folding. The stuff that's upside down will look just fine after you fold it.

End

How to Create a Banner

If someone in your office just won a Nobel prize, you should celebrate. At home, perhaps a family member or a neighbor just returned from the Oscar awards clutching her statue.

The celebration is much more fun with a banner. Luckily, you don't have to draw one (banners are a lot of work) because you have Publisher.

Begin

1 Choose Banner

Choose **File**, **New** from the **menu bar** to bring up the Catalog. (The Catalog appears automatically if you're just opening Publisher.) Choose **Banners** from the **Publications by Wizard** tab to expand the list of banners.

2 Choose a Specific Banner

Select the type of banner you want. There's only one of each, so as soon as you make your selection, the appropriate sample is selected in the right pane. Choose **Start Wizard**.

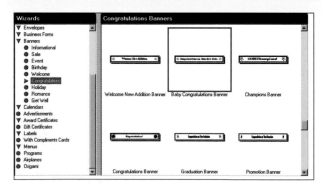

3 Design the Banner

Choose **Next** in the **wizard** pane to tell the wizard how long you want your banner to be. (Choose **Custom** to enter a length that isn't listed.) Then choose **Next** to continue instructing the wizard. Answer the other questions about height, the placement of graphics, and whether you want a border.

4 Choose Finish

Choose **Finish** when you've completed the wizard's questionnaire and hide the wizard so you can work on your banner. You can change the text, the graphics, or the border.

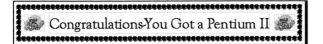

5 Choose Print

Banners are printed on multiple pieces of paper. Choose **File**, **Print** from the **menu bar**. When the **Print** dialog box opens, choose **Tile Printing Options**.

6 Select Options

Check the paper use in the **Poster and Banner Printing Options** dialog box. If only a tiny portion of the last piece of paper is being used, you can reduce the size of the overlap to eliminate it. (Most of the time it's best to leave everything the way Publisher set it up.) Choose **OK** to return to the **Print** dialog box. Print your banner, get out the tape or glue, and put it together.

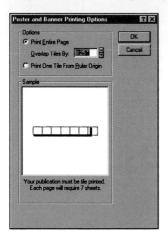

How-To Hints

Add a Personal Touch

Every banner I've ever created in Publisher or helped clients create had decorations added after it was printed and assembled. Having people sign their names (along with a sweet or funny sentiment) is part of the fun of banners.

End

3

How to Build an Airplane

Don't laugh. Think about it: An airplane isn't just a toy; it can be a great marketing device. Send an airplane to your customers to announce your new catalog, a price reduction, a new phone number (or email address).

Or, for personal messages, send an airplane to announce a new address; use it as a greeting card.

Begin

1 Choose Airplanes

Open the Catalog and choose **Airplanes** (in the Publications by Wizard tab) to see the available selections. Select the airplane you want to create and choose **Start Wizard**.

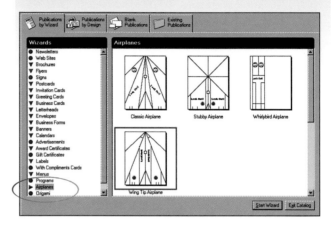

2 Choose Next

Choose **Next** in the **wizard** pane to begin designing the colors (use black and white if you're going to print on colored paper) and making other decisions.

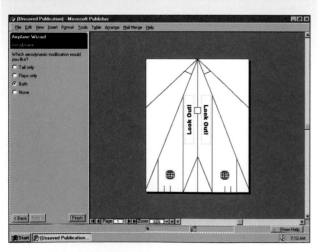

3 Customize Airplane Text

Choose **Finish** and then hide the wizard to begin working on your design. Start by selecting a text frame and replacing the placeholder text with your own words. Notice that the copyfitting feature is turned on, so the font gets smaller if you use more words. (Learn about copyfitting text in Task 2, "How to Copyfit," in Chapter 5.)

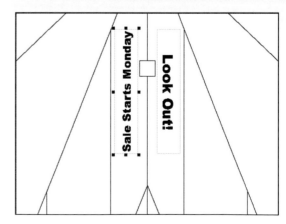

4 Customize Airplane Graphics

Double-click the picture frames to replace the clip art with a design of your own choosing. There is information about clip art in Task 7, "How to Insert Clip Art," in Chapter 3.

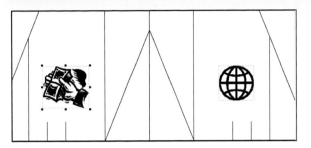

5 Customize Folding Instructions

Move to the second page if you want to add a personal note in the instructions.

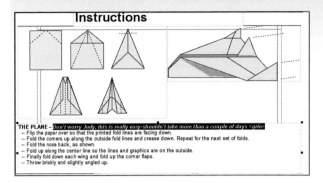

6 Print Airplane

Click the **Print** icon on the **Standard** toolbar to print your airplane and its instructions.

Click

End

How-To Hints

Add Pizzazz to Your Aircraft with Nifty Paper

Airplanes are more fun if you use special paper, especially shiny (even metallic) paper.

TASK **4**

How to Create Origami

Origami is the ancient Japanese art of folding a piece of paper so that it becomes a recognizable object. Most of the time origami produces graceful paper sculptures of birds, but you can build almost anything you want to—unless you don't know the art and have to rely on the choices available in Publisher.

This is another specialty publication that has multiple uses. You can create origami for fun, as greeting cards, or as a marketing publication.

Begin

1 Choose Origami

Choose **Origami** from the Catalog (in the **Publications by Wizard** tab) and then select the specific origami shape you want to create. Choose **Start Wizard** to begin.

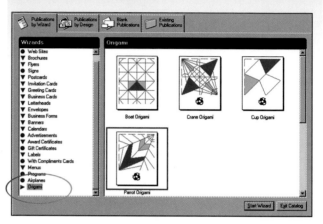

2 Click Next

Click **Next** in the **wizard** pane to configure your publication. The only decision to make in Origami is the color scheme. The default is usually muted colors (traditional with this art), but you might want to use a company's company logo colors or some other more colorful scheme.

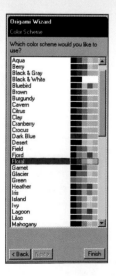

3 Choose Finish

Choose **Finish** and then hide the wizard so you can begin working on your origami publication. Only the boat origami uses the entire piece of paper, so if you've selected anything else you see a second graphic at the bottom of your page.

4 Customize Origami

Select the extra design element and change the art work (perhaps you want to insert the company logo).

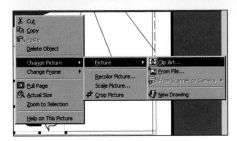

5 Customize Folding Instructions

The second page of the origami publication contains directions for folding. These are usually graphic frames, so the only way to personalize this page is to add a small text frame if there's room for it. Don't disturb the size or shape of the instructions—they're hard enough to follow when they're the proper size.

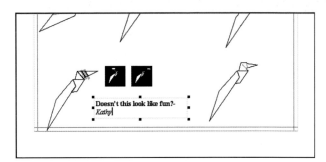

6 Click Print

Click the **Print** icon on the **Standard** toolbar to print your origami publication.

Click

End

How-To Hints

Use Plain Paper

Origami folds better if the paper you use isn't slick or coated. Use the inexpensive laser/copier paper for best results.

TASK 5

How to Create Calendars

Sending calendars to your customers is a great idea. Every time the customer enters an appointment or checks the date, there's a reminder of your company.

Calendars are really effective when you add all sorts of personal touches and send them to friends and relatives.

Begin

1 Choose a Calendar

Open the Catalog and click the **Calendars** entry to expand it. Then select **Full Page** or **Wallet Size**. In the right pane, select the layout you want to use and then choose **Start Wizard**.

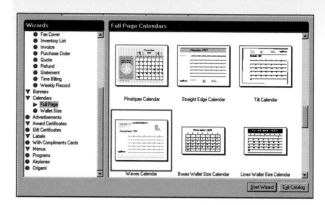

2 Configure the Calendar

Click **Next** in the **wizard** pane to begin answering the configuration questions. You start by selecting a color scheme; the remaining options depend on the calendar type you chose. You'll have to tell Publisher what dates you need on the calendar.

3 Adding a Schedule of Events

The wizard offers to add a schedule of events to your calendar, which is a good idea if you have events. A blank event section looks silly, so choose **No** if you don't have any events.

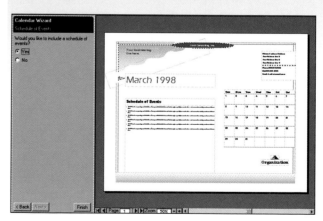

4 Customizing Your Calendar

Choose **Finish** and hide the wizard to begin working on your publication. Select the frames you need to work in and change the text as necessary. For example, if you have a schedule of events for the month the calendar covers, add them to the schedule frame. Notice that the schedule is a bullet list. (Read all about creating bullet lists in Task 6, "How to Create Lists," in Chapter 2.)

Schedule of Events

- Date – Describe an upcoming event in detail here. You may want to include the time and location or give a special phone number where readers can reach a contact person for more information.

- Date – Describe an upcoming event in detail here. You may want to include the time and location or give a special phone number where readers can reach a contact person for more information.

- Date – Describe an upcoming event in detail here. You may want to include the time and location or give a special phone number where readers can reach a contact person for more information.

- Date – Describe an upcoming event in detail here. You may want to include the time and location or give a special phone number where readers can reach a contact person for more information.

- Date – Describe an upcoming event in detail here. You may want to include the time and location or give a special phone number where readers can reach a contact person for more information.

- Date – Describe an upcoming event in detail here. You may want to include the time and location or give a special phone number where readers can reach a contact person for more information.

5 Adding Special Dates

It's a good idea to annotate special dates right on the date block, which is a text frame.

1	2	3	4	5	6	7
8	9	10	11	12 My Birth-day	13	14
15	16	17	18	19	20	21
22	23	24	25 Last Day for Discounts	26	27	28

6 Printing Your Calendar

Click the **Print** icon on the **Standard** toolbar to print your calendar.

File Edit View Insert Format Tools Table Arrange Mail Merge Help

Click

End

How-To Hints

Monthly Calendars Have Room to Add Text

If you want to personalize dates, choose a monthly calendar instead of a yearly calendar.

How to Get Presents

A nifty trick is to enter your own birthday on calendars you send to friends and relatives.

How to Create Signs

I have a friend with a two-car garage and three cars in the family. Parking on the driveway in front of the garage always creates a problem. She has a sign that says Park Here and Die. You can't buy signs like that; you have to make them.

You probably need signs that are less original, but whether you need to put up notices for employees, place signs on rooms to indicate their numbers or names, or warn people that you have a killer cat, you can save money by creating your own signs.

Begin

1 Choose Signs

In the Catalog, choose **Signs** (in the **Publications by Wizard** tab) and then scroll through the signs in the right pane to find the style that comes closest to your own needs; then choose **Start Wizard**.

2 Select a Color Scheme

Click **Next** in the **wizard** pane to get started. The only decision the wizard requests of you is the color scheme. Select the hues you want to use and click **Finish**; then hide the wizard so you can work on your sign.

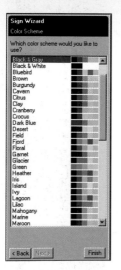

3 Ungroup Sign Elements

Some elements in the sign are grouped. If you want to change one element in the group, click the **Ungroup Objects** button to separate the elements. Learn about working with groups by reading Task 13, "How to Group and Ungroup Objects," in Chapter 3.

4 Customizing the Graphics

Change the picture in a graphic frame by double-clicking it and selecting new art work.

5 Customizing the Text

Change text by selecting the text frame and making the appropriate edits.

6 Click Print

Click the **Print** button on the **Standard** toolbar to print your sign.

Click

End

How-To Hints

Print Without Turning the Paper Around the Rollers

If you use heavier paper for your signs, it's a good idea to either go to your printer and push whatever buttons have to be pushed or open whatever panels have to be opened to provide a straight-through path for the paper. If your printer cannot print without turning the paper, print on regular paper and then glue the paper to a heavier material.

How to Create Ads

If you're in business, you probably advertise that business. If you buy space in a newspaper or magazine, you have to provide the ad (or pay the paper or magazine to produce one, which is frequently not worth the money).

Use Publisher to create your ads—you'll end up with a polished, professional look without paying an agency big bucks.

Begin

1 Choose Advertisements

In the Catalog, choose **Advertisements** (in the **Publications by Wizard** tab) and then scroll through the designs in the right pane to find the one that comes closest to the format you need.

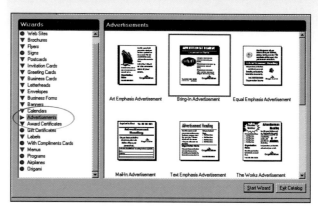

2 Choose Ad Size

Choose **Start Wizard** to begin configuring your ad. The first wizard question is about the ad's size; standard sizes are offered. If the space you bought doesn't match the wizard's choices, click the **Custom** button to open the **Page Setup** dialog box, which has the **Special Size** option selected.

3 Customize Ad Size

Enter the **Width** and **Height** you need and choose **OK**.

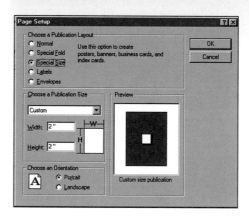

4 Answer the Wizard's Questions

Choose **Next** in the **wizard** pane to continue answering questions about your design, choosing **Next** after you complete each answer. If you have a *logo sheet* (a set of printed logos), tell the wizard to leave a placeholder and give the logo to the newspaper separately, or paste it on your printout. (The logo placeholder is the little **pyramid** graphic.) If your advertisement is small, you can print multiple copies (which is useful if you're buying space in multiple publications).

5 Customize Ad

Choose **Finish** and hide the wizard to start working on your ad. Select frames and replace the placeholder contents with your own contents.

6 Print Ad

Click the **Print** button on the **Standard** toolbar to produce a printed ad. It's a good idea to use coated paper to make sure the image stays crisp as it goes through production (and gets printed on the cheap paper used by newspapers).

Click

End

How-To Hints

Black and White

Design ads in black and white, even if the printed ad will be colorized—the paper's/magazine's Production Department will handle the colorization. Provide color swatches or chips. (There are books with standard colors with tear-out squares you can give to the Production Department.)

How to Create Business Forms

Some businesses have an incredible amount of forms, (although probably nobody has as many as the government). It can be expensive to design and print forms. To top it off, every time there's a change in company policy, there's a good chance there has to be a change in some form.

Businesses that don't have forms aren't in better shape because of that lack. It means that expense accounts are handed in by putting rubber bands around receipts; sales orders are scribbled on Post-It Notes (or napkins, if the sale was made at lunch).

The solution? Create forms in Publisher. You'll have all the forms you need for good record keeping, and you won't spend a fortune on printing.

Begin

1 Choose Business Forms

In the Catalog, click **Business Forms** (on the **Publications by Wizard** tab) to expand the listing of available forms. Select the type of form you need, and then choose a design from the right pane. Click the **Start Wizard** button to begin designing your form.

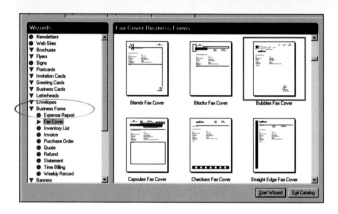

2 Design Forms Through Wizards

Choose **Next** and answer the wizard's questions (which vary, depending on the form you chose); choose **Finish** and hide the wizard so you can work on the publication.

3 Click Publications by Design Tab

If you need a variety of forms, move to the Catalog's **Publications by Design** tab. Choose a design that pleases you and then choose the forms you need. They'll all have the same design, which is a nice, professional approach.

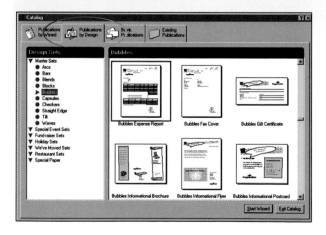

4 Customize Forms

Edit the form, adding or changing the text and graphics that Publisher provides.

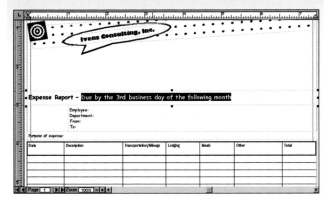

5 Print Forms

Print the form and distribute it, or send it to your printer for outside printing.

Click

End

How-To Hints

Special Needs May Require an Outside Printer

It's not always possible to print the forms you design in Publisher in-house, especially if you use non-standard paper, need duplicate copies (pink, white, and so on), or want the forms bound into a pad. However, creating the design for the printer (called a _mechanical_ or a _camera-ready_ hard copy) can save you money and time.

How to Use Special Paper

Publisher provides information about obtaining special, preprinted paper (with color swatches or patterns). This is a great way to get colorful designs on your publications without having to use an outside printing service.

The company that provides the templates and designs is PaperDirect, which has a catalog available if you want to see all the paper stock available; the catalog items are more numerous than the designs displayed in Publisher. The catalog is in your Publisher 98 package.

Begin

1 Choose Special Paper

The quickest way to see the special paper offerings is to move to the **Publications by Design** tab in the Catalog and select **Special Paper**. Choose a design and then select a form from the right pane. Click **Start Wizard** to begin working on the form.

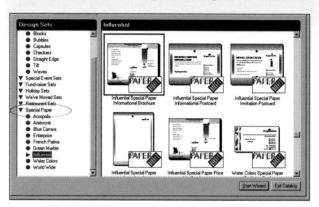

2 Design Through Wizard's Questions

Answer the wizard's questions and then click **Finish**; hide the wizard so you can work on the publication.

3 Press Ctrl+M for Background Design

The text and graphic frames on the publication page are carefully positioned so you don't print over the designs on the paper. (Publisher uses the background page to hold the paper design; you can press **Ctrl+M** to see it.) See Task 6, "How to Create Background Elements," in Chapter 4 for information on using the background.

4 Customize Special Paper

Either select text frames to add or change text or format the text. If there are graphic images on the form, double-click them to put a different graphic in the frame.

5 Print Special Paper

Put the special paper into your printer's paper tray. Choose **File**, **Print** to bring up the **Print** dialog box. Specify the number of copies you need and press **OK**.

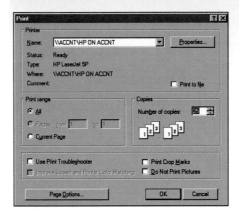

End

How-To Hints

You Can Use any Pre-Designed Paper

If you have your own source of predesigned paper stock, you can adjust the PaperDirect templates you find in Publisher to fit the patterns or use a blank publication template and design your own.

Task

8

Printing Your Publication

*P*rinting a publication is frequently far more complicated than printing a document from your word processor. In fact, there will be many occasions in which you'll find your printer just won't do an adequate job—you'll want the services of a professional printing company.

If your publication requires special handling as it is sent to your own printer, Publisher helps you make the right decisions and choose the right options.

If you have to use an outside company, Publisher walks you through the process so the experience doesn't turn into a nightmare.

In this chapter you learn how to print your publication in-house and out-of-house. ●

TASK *1*

How to Print Your Publication

After you've done all the work involved in creating a masterpiece of a publication, you'll certainly want people to read it. Unless you're planning to gather all those people in front of your monitor, you have to print it.

Begin

1 Quickly Print the Publication

To send your publication to your printer quickly and with no muss, no fuss, click the **Print** button on the **Standard** toolbar. It's quick, but there is a downside—you have no choices about what pages to print or which printer to use. The entire publication prints to the currently selected printer. (Or, even worse, if you printed with the Print dialog box before you click the Print button, the settings you left behind are used for this print job.)

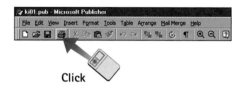

Click

2 Configure the Printer

You can change the printer options to match your publication, including resolution, paper, graphics, and so on. Choose **File**, **Print Setup** from the **menu bar** to see the **Print Setup** dialog box, where you can change the paper size and the tray. Click the **Properties** button to make any needed adjustments to the printer's configuration. (Each printer has its own set of properties.)

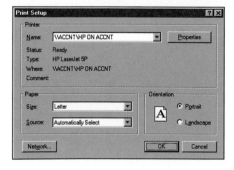

3 Set Printer Options

Press **Ctrl+P** to open the **Print** dialog box, so you can set the printing options. Choose the pages you want to print, the number of copies, and so on. You can change printers if you have more than one printer available.

4 Print to File

You can select **Print to File** to create a file copy of the print job; you can take that copy to another printer. Publisher asks for a filename. This is useful for printing to a more powerful printer (especially if you don't have a color printer). This only works if you install that printer's drivers on your computer. Don't worry, it's okay to lie to your computer and tell it you have a powerful printer. Select that printer in the **Print** dialog box, print to a file, and take the file to a computer that really has that printer.

5 Print the Publication

Choose **OK** on the **Print** dialog box to send your publication to the printer. If your publication is large and has a lot of graphics, you'll probably have to wait a bit to see the printed image. This is normal, and you shouldn't assume that there's a problem.

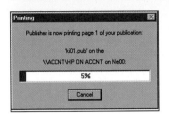

6 Troubleshoot Printing

Select **Use Print Troubleshooter** on the **Print** dialog box; that tells Publisher to help you with printing if there are any problems. As soon as your publication is sent to the printer, the **Print Troubleshooter** opens. Select any problem that matches the problem you encountered, and Publisher walks you through suggestions and hints to resolve it.

How-To Hints

Install Lots of Printers

I've installed a slew of fake printers on my computer. When I need the capabilities of one of those printers I select it and print to a file. Of course, I have to call around to find somebody who really owns that printer, but I'm generally successful. You can do the same thing, by telling your operating system to install the drivers for a particular printer as if that printer was really connected to your computer. Your operating system cheerfully complies. It can't peek through the monitor and look around, so you'll never see a message that says "liar, liar, you don't really have that printer." This works because operating systems let you install multiple printers to the same port (I usually use LPT1). Just be careful that none of your fake printers are designated as the default printer for your computer.

End

TASK *2*

How to Print Special Publications

Many of Publisher's publications require special printing techniques. For example, your publication may need a special paper size or it may be extremely small (such as a business card or a postcard). If so, you need to plan and set up the printing process.

If your publication is configured for a size that's smaller than the standard letter paper, you can either feed that paper into the printer or print on letter paper. If you choose the latter, you must print crop marks so you'll know where to cut the paper.

2 Printing to Unique Paper Sizes

If you want to print directly on the paper that matches the size of your publication, choose **Properties** in the **Print** dialog box and select the paper size. If your printer doesn't offer the size you need, you may be able to enter a custom size (if not, choose the closest size). If the printer doesn't have a paper tray for the size you need, choose the manual feed option.

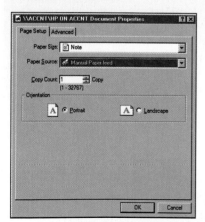

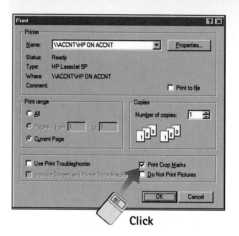

Begin

1 Printing on Regular Paper

Press **Ctrl+P** to open the **Print** dialog box and select **Print Crop Marks**. Use the crop marks to cut the paper evenly. For business cards, take the printout to a quick copy shop or printer. Pick the paper stock and colors you want and the printer will do the rest.

Click

3 Printing Multiple Business Cards

If you want to print a bunch of business cards yourself, choose **Page Options** from the **Print** dialog box to open the **Page Options** dialog box. Select **Print multiple copies per sheet**, then choose **OK** to return to the **Print** dialog box. Select **Print Crop Marks** and click **OK** to print; use the crop marks to cut.

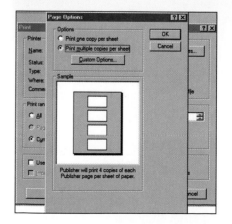

4 Configuring Multiple Cards

You can configure the way multiple cards are printed (business cards, placecards, or any other very small publication). Open the **Page Options** dialog box as described in Step 3 and choose **Custom Options**. In the **Custom Options** dialog box, change the margins and the *gaps* (the space between each printed section). You may have to experiment a bit, but usually this makes printing more economical.

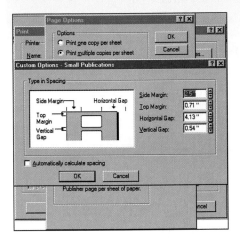

5 Printing a Draft Copy

If you want to see what your layout looks like in print, you can speed printing by skipping the pictures. Open the **Print** dialog box and select **Do Not Print Pictures**. The printed copy will indicate the placement of all the pictures with dotted lines.

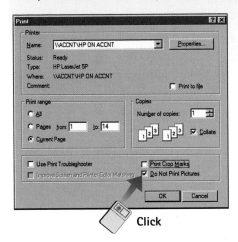

Click

6 Other Tricks for Quick Printing

There are other ways to speed printing for all the draft copies you must print. Open the **Print** dialog box and choose **Properties**. Change the resolution to a lower number—this speeds printing substantially. (Don't forget to skip the pictures.)

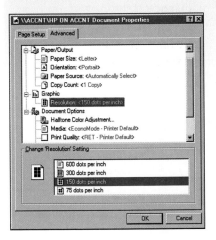

How-To Hints

Use Draft Printing to Create a Paste-Up

You can also use the draft printing technique described in Step 5 to paste pictures in those dotted lines and take the printout to a professional printer. If you prefer not to, indicate the picture number with a pencil mark and then mark the real pictures with the corresponding numbers. (Let the printer handle the paste-up.)

End

How to Use an Outside Printing Service

Some of your publications will be printed by an outside printing service, which can provide all the professional services you need. Annual reports, bound publications, and other major publishing projects should be printed professionally.

You must provide your printing service with all the necessary information. In order to do that, you must have directions from the service about the kind of file they expect and the sort of specific instructions they need.

Begin

1 Print the Checklist

Publisher provides a terrific checklist that you should use to work out the details with your printing service. It covers all the details you have to discuss. You can print it through the Help files. Click the **Show Index** button and enter **printing service checklist** in the **Index** keyword box. A **Help** box opens as soon as you finish typing. Click where indicated to print a copy of the checklist. Click **Done** to close the **Help** box and then the **Hide Help** button.

2 Begin Preparing Your File

Choose **File, Prepare File for Printing Service, Set Up Publication** from the **menu bar**.

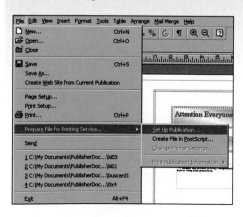

3 Preparing for Full Color Printing

If your publication is to be printed in full color, select **Full color** in the **Set Up Publication** dialog box.

4 Specify the Color Printer

Choose **Next** to move to the next window, where you're asked to select the printer your outside service will use for this job. Choose **Use Publisher's commercial printer driver** (which supports almost all of the printers used by commercial printers), then choose **Done**.

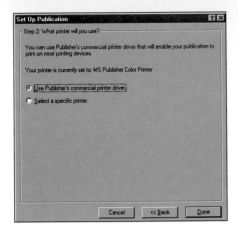

5 Preparing for Spot Color Printing

If you're planning on spot color printing, choose **Spot colors** in the **Set Up Publication** dialog box. Select the color (or colors, if you want two spot colors). Choose **Next** to select a printer. (Use the commercial printer from Publisher as discussed in Step 4.) Choose **Next** again to set printing options.

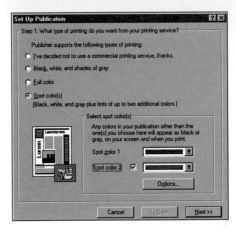

6 Set the Spot Color Options

Most printing services require you to set options for extra paper sizes (that means it's expected that the paper used is larger than the final publication, in order to print the color all the way to the edge of the publication). In addition, all printing services expect the publication to be configured for printing marks. Check with your printing service before selecting these options, however. Choose **Done** when all these steps have been completed. When you return to the **Publisher** window, notice that your publication is displaying in black and white (and gray if you used colors).

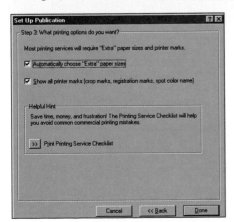

Continues

7 Set Up a PostScript File

If your printing service is using a PostScript printer, you must prepare the file for them. For standard PostScript printing, choose **File**, **Prepare For Printing Service**, **Create File in PostScript**.

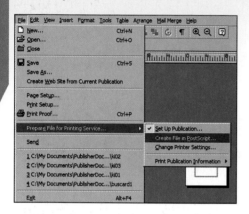

8 Set Up the PostScript Printer

Select a **PostScript Printer** in the **Print** dialog box. If you don't have one, choose either the **MS Publisher Imagesetter** (for black-and-white or spot color printing) or the **MS Publisher Color Printer** (for full-color printing).

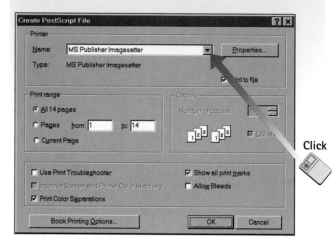

Click

9 Set Up the PostScript Features

Click **Properties** on the **Print** dialog box and move to the **Properties** dialog box's **PostScript** tab. Select **PostScript (optimize for portability-ADSC)**. Choose **OK** to return to the **Print** dialog box.

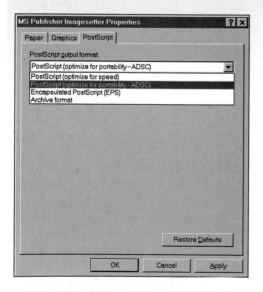

10 Print to a Disk File

Be sure that **Print to file** is selected in the **Print** dialog box and then choose **OK**. When the **Print To File** dialog box opens, enter a **File name** (Publisher adds the extension **.prn** automatically). Choose **OK** to have Publisher print the file to your disk. Copy the file to a floppy disk if it is small enough. Otherwise, try compressing the file with a program like WinZip to make it small enough for a floppy disk, or send the file via email.

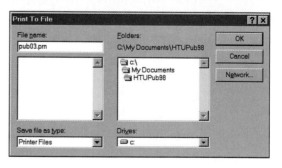

⑪ Prepare a Commercial Printer File

If your printing service needs different settings than those discussed in the previous steps, choose **File**, **Prepare File for Printing Service**, **Change Printer Settings**.

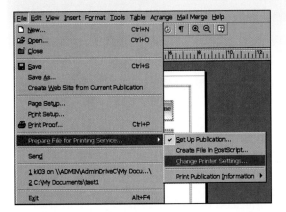

⑫ Configure the Printer Settings

Select the appropriate printer, and then choose **Properties**; make changes to the settings as your printing service requires. For example, Publisher doesn't support 1200dpi resolution if you're printing in full color, so you have to change the printer to the **MS Publisher Color Printer**, and change the file output to **EPS** (Encapsulated PostScript). Press **OK** and perform Step 10.

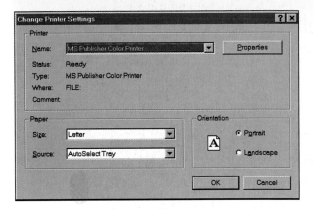

⑬ Print a Proof

You need a proof copy of your publication to show to the printing service (feel free to write notes on it). A *proof copy* is a copy of your publication that is composed and configured on the printing service's printer (the MS Publisher printer) and printed to your regular printer. This is a complicated process, so it may take a few moments to print. Choose **File**, **Print Proof** from the **File** menu to open the **Print** dialog box. Everything should be set properly, so choose **OK**.

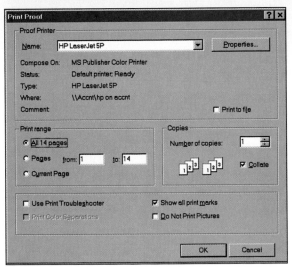

End

How-To Hints

Installing Publisher's Commercial Printer

If you receive an error message about the commercial printer when you try to set up your publication for outside printing, it means you didn't install the commercial printer when you installed Publisher. Start the Publisher 98 setup again and choose **Add/Remove** in the **Setup** dialog box. Select the **Publisher's Commercial Printer Drivers** box and click **Continue**. Publisher takes care of the rest and informs you when the installation is complete.

Understanding Spot Color Printing

Spot color is a process in which your publication is put through the printing process one time for each color. In order to do this, your printing service must be able to create *color separations* (a technical process that your printing service will understand when you ask about it).

Project

Project 3

Here's a challenge: You work in the Human Resources Department of the NeverClose Convenience Shop and Gas Station chain, and there's a desperate need for cashiers. Your boss told you to place a large ad in the local paper as well as on the Web. (Customers visit your Web site because you have contests in the stores that require a Web visit in order to enter the contest.) The company Webmaster told you he's too busy to create the Web page and told you to design the ad and then convert it to a Web page. The Advertising Department told you it bought newspaper space requiring an ad that's 13" high by 7.5" wide. Let's go!

1 Start with a Blank Page

When Publisher opens to the Catalog, choose **Exit Catalog** to get to a blank page—you're doing this one from scratch.

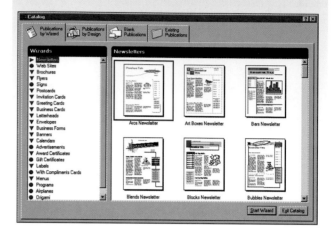

2 Set Up the Page

To tell Publisher about the paper's unusual size, choose **File**, **Page Setup** from the **menu bar**.

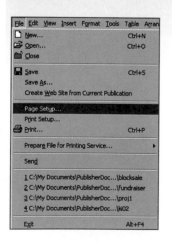

3 Specify the Page Size

Select **Special Size** in the **Page Setup** dialog box. Specify a **Width** of **8.5"** and a **Height** of **14"** to allow for the margins your printer needs. (Laser printers can't print to the edge of the paper.) Click **OK**.

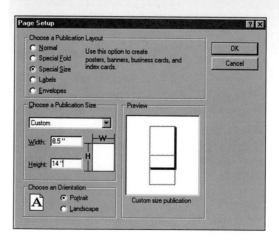

4 Create a Headline

Click the **Text Frame Tool** button on the **Objects** toolbar and drag a frame across the top of the page to hold a headline. Enter your headline text. (Press **F9** to zoom in so you can see what you're typing as you enter your text.)

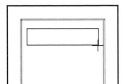

5 Format the Headline

Format the headline using the tools on the **Formatting** toolbar. Make the font larger (you might want to choose a different font), and make the text **Bold**, *Italic*, or both. Don't forget to use the **Center** button to align the text in the middle of the frame.

6 Add Body Copy

Add another text frame to use for the body copy you need. This example has a list, so select the text that should be listed and click the **Bullets** button on the **Formatting** toolbar.

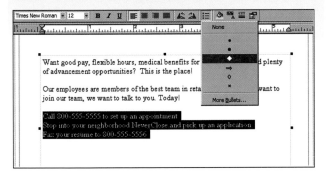

7 Tweak Line Spacing

Make the list look more professional by tweaking the spacing between lines. Select the bullet list and choose **Format**, **Line Spacing**. Use the **Line Spacing** dialog box options to loosen up the spacing so that the list is easier to read. Choose **OK**.

Continues

8 Add Graphics or Text

Add graphics and text as necessary. If you put a graphic frame in a text frame, you must move or resize the graphic frame to make sure the text wraps properly.

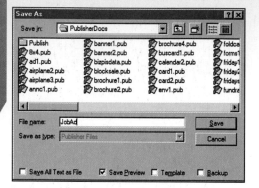

9 Save Your Publication

Save the publication by clicking the **Save** button on the **Standard** toolbar. The first time you save, a **Save As** dialog box opens so you can name the document; choose **Save** after you do so. Hereafter, click the **Save** button on the **Standard** toolbar each time you add another element so everything you do is saved.

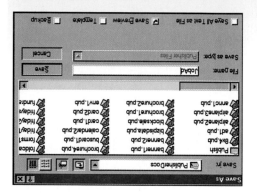

10 Begin Web Conversion

To begin the Web conversion of this copy of your publication, choose **File, Create Web Site from Current Publication**.

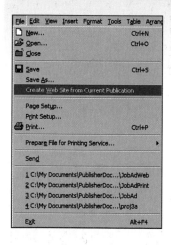

11 Run the Design Checker

Publisher displays a dialog box offering to run the Design Checker. Click **Yes** so your publication can be checked for any problems that may occur when it's converted for the Web. When the Design Checker asks which pages to check, choose **All** and click **OK**.

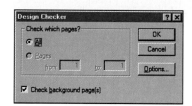

12 Check the Download Time

Fix or **Ignore** any problems the Design Checker finds. (After the design check is complete, you're asked if you want to check the download time for your Web page. Click **Yes** to determine whether your file is so large that it will take a long time to load. If it seems too large, eliminate some graphic images.)

13 Add Links

Now that you have a Web publication, you should give readers a way to navigate to other places on your Web site. Select the text that you want to use as a hyperlink, and then choose **Insert**, **Hyperlink** from the **menu bar**.

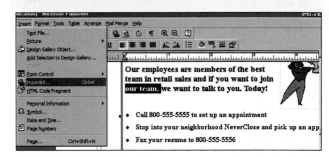

14 Enter Hyperlink Addresses

Fill out the appropriate options in the **Hyperlink** dialog box (check with your Webmaster). Choose **OK**.

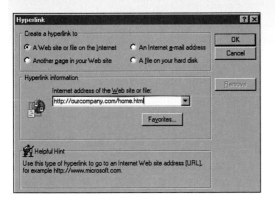

15 Check Your Links

Check the linked text on the page to make sure it's underlined, which indicates a link. Position your mouse over the text to make sure the link information that's displayed in the ScreenTip is correct.

> Our employees are members of the best team in retail sales and if you want to join our team, we want to talk to you. Today!
>
> http://ourcompany.com/home.html
>
> Call 800-555-5555 to set up an appointment

Continues ➤

16 Save an Extra Copy

Here's a trick I learned: Save this file again under a different name so you have a copy of your publication as it's set up for the Web. Later, when you save it as a Web file (an HTML file), you don't have a chance to give it a new name. This way you'll have a file without links and underlined text for your printed copy, and another file with the Web features. Choose **File**, **Save As** from the **menu bar** and use a filename that indicates the publication is "Web ready."

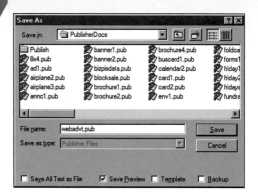

17 Preview Your Site

Aren't you dying to know what this publication will look like when Web visitors see it? You can preview by choosing **File**, **Web Site Preview** from the **menu bar**.

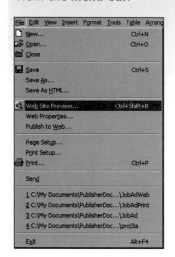

18 Check Your Links

Your browser launches and your Web page is displayed in the **browser** window. Check your hyperlinks by positioning your mouse pointer over the hyperlink; your pointer should turn into a hand. Close the browser to return to your **Publisher** window, where you can make any changes you feel are necessary.

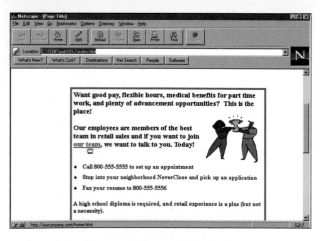

19 Convert to HTML

A standard Publisher file format doesn't work on the Web, so you must save your file as an HTML file. Choose **File**, **Save as HTML** from the **menu bar**. When the **Save as HTML** dialog box opens, you'll see that Publisher has created a subfolder named **Publish** to hold your converted files. Choose **OK** to use that folder. Notice that you're not asked for a filename (which is why I told you to save it as a different file in Step 16; now you can still retrieve it if you want to make changes to this Web-oriented file).

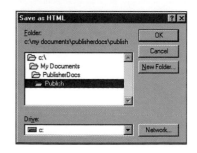

20 Print to Paper

Now you must print your original (non-Web) publication for the newspaper ad. (You could have done this earlier, before you converted the publication to a Web document, but it's being done now in this case.) Click the **Open** button on the **Standard** toolbar and double-click the filename you originally gave this publication (before you saved it under a different filename after converting it). The publication (sans hyperlinks) opens in your **Publisher** window.

21 Configure Your Printer

Press **Ctrl+P** to bring up the **Print** dialog box. Because this paper is larger than standard, click the **Properties** button to configure the printer for legal paper. (Different printers have different methods for accomplishing this, and you may have to change the tray assignment or choose manual feed.) Choose **OK** to print your publication.

End

Glossary

A–B

background page   A virtual page that holds elements that you want repeated on every page of your publication.

bleed   Printing past the edge of a margin; used mainly to ensure that color graphics or backgrounds reach the edge of the finished page.

C

camera–ready   A printed document that's ready for an outside printing service to print. The name comes from the fact that a camera is used to take a picture and then use the negative for printing.

Clip Gallery   A program that contains clip art, pictures, sound files, and video clips that can be used in publications.

copyfit   Size text to fit into a specific amount of space (the space is defined as a frame in Publisher).

D–E–F

Design Gallery   A collection of special predesigned and preformatted elements you can add to a publication.

dialog box   An information box that appears when the software needs input from the user.

G

gutter   The space on a page left blank for binding. (The left edge of a right page, the right edge of a left page.)

H–I

hard copy   Computer jargon for a printed copy of a document file.

J

justification   Aligning text so that it fills the area between the left and right margins.

K

kerning   Changing the size of spaces between specific pairs of characters.

L

layout guides   Guide lines you put on the background page, representing boundaries for all pages in your publication. You can also use these guide lines to align objects.

leading   (Pronounced *ledding*) The spacing between lines.

M–N

mechanical   Printing term for finished art work that's ready to be processed by a printer. See also *camera-ready*.

O–P

placeholder text   Text that is inserted automatically in a text frame. It is replaced by your own text.

printer properties   Information about your printer and its capabilities. To see the properties, choose **Settings**, **Printers** from the **Start** menu and right-click the icon for your printer. Choose **Properties** from the **shortcut menu** to see the **Properties** dialog box.

Q–R

ruler guides   Guide lines representing ruler positions that you place on a page in order to align objects.

S

scratch area   The portion of the **Publisher** window outside the page display. Use the scratch area to "park" frames you want to move to another page.

ScreenTips   Notes displayed on your screen to explain a function or feature.

Snap To   A feature that forces objects to a specific position on a page by making them snap to a guide line.

T–U–V

Text Overflow icon   A button at the bottom of a text frame; indicates there is additional text in the frame that is not currently seen because the frame isn't large enough to display it.

tracking   Changing the size of the spaces between characters.

W–X–Y–Z

watermark   A pale element placed in the background of a document page. Used for graphics or special text.

Index

Body Text Fonts

Arial
The quick brown fox jumps over the lazy dog 1234567890

Arial Narrow
The quick brown fox jumps over the lazy dog 1234567890

Arial Rounded MT Bold
The quick brown fox jumps over the lazy dog 1234567890

Baskerville Old Face
The quick brown fox jumps over the lazy dog 1234567890

Bell MT
The quick brown fox jumps over the lazy dog 1234567890

Book Antiqua
The quick brown fox jumps over the lazy dog 1234567890

Bookman Old Style
The quick brown fox jumps over the lazy dog 1234567890

Calisto MT
The quick brown fox jumps over the lazy dog 1234567890

Centaur
The quick brown fox jumps over the lazy dog 1234567890

Century Schoolbook
The quick brown fox jumps over the lazy dog 1234567890

Comic Sans MS
The quick brown fox jumps over the lazy dog 1234567890

Courier New
The quick brown fox jumps over the lazy dog 1234567890

Eras Medium ITC
The quick brown fox jumps over the lazy dog 1234567890

Footlight MT Light
The quick brown fox jumps over the lazy dog 1234567890

Franklin Gothic Book
The quick brown fox jumps over the lazy dog 1234567890

Garamond
The quick brown fox jumps over the lazy dog 1234567890

Georgia
The quick brown fox jumps over the lazy dog 1234567890

Gill Sans MT
The quick brown fox jumps over the lazy dog 1234567890

Goudy Old Style
The quick brown fox jumps over the lazy dog 1234567890

Lucida Bright
The quick brown fox jumps over the lazy dog 1234567890

Lucida Sans
The quick brown fox jumps over the lazy dog 1234567890

Lucida Sans Typewriter
The quick brown fox jumps over the lazy dog 1234567890

Maiandra GD
The quick brown fox jumps over the lazy dog 1234567890

Modern No. 20
The quick brown fox jumps over the lazy dog 1234567890

Perpetua
The quick brown fox jumps over the lazy dog 1234567890

Tahoma
The quick brown fox jumps over the lazy dog 1234567890

Times New Roman
The quick brown fox jumps over the lazy dog 1234567890

Trebuchet MS
The quick brown fox jumps over the lazy dog 1234567890

Tw Cen MT
The quick brown fox jumps over the lazy dog 1234567890

Verdana
The quick brown fox jumps over the lazy dog 1234567890

Impact Fonts

Arial Black
The quick brown fox jumps over the lazy dog 1234567890

Bernard MT Condensed
The quick brown fox jumps over the lazy dog 1234567890

Bauhaus 93
The quick brown fox jumps over the lazy dog 1234567890

Brittanic Bold
The quick brown fox jumps over the lazy dog 1234567890

Broadway
The quick brown fox jumps over the lazy dog 1234567890

Cooper Black
The quick brown fox jumps over the lazy dog 1234567890

Copperplate Gothic
THE QUICK BROWN FOX JUMPS OVER THE LAZY DOG 1234567890

Elephant
The quick brown fox jumps over the lazy dog 1234567890

Eras Bold ITC
The quick brown fox jumps over the lazy dog 1234567890

Franklin Gothic Heavy
The quick brown fox jumps over the lazy dog 1234567890

Gill Sans Ultra Bold
The quick brown fox jumps over the lazy dog 1234567890

Haettenschweiler
The quick brown fox jumps over the lazy dog 1234567890

Impact
The quick brown fox jumps over the lazy dog 1234567890

Matura MT Script Capitals
The quick brown fox jumps over the lazy dog 1234567890

Playbill
The quick brown fox jumps over the lazy dog 1234567890

Rockwell Extra Bold
The quick brown fox jumps over the lazy dog 1234567890

Wide Latin
The quick brown fox jumps over the lazy dog 1234567890

Display Fonts

ALGERIAN
THE QUICK BROWN FOX JUMPS OVER THE LAZY DOG 1234567890

Blackadder ITC
The quick brown fox jumps over the lazy dog 1234567890

Bradley Hand ITC
The quick brown fox jumps over the lazy dog 1234567890

Brush Script MT
The quick brown fox jumps over the lazy dog 1234567890

CASTELLAR
THE QUICK BROWN FOX JUMPS OVER THE LAZY DOG 1234567890

Chiller
The quick brown fox jumps over the lazy dog 1234567890

Colonna MT
The quick brown fox jumps over the lazy dog 1234567890

Curlz MT
The quick brown fox jumps over the lazy dog 1234567890

Edwardian Script ITC
The quick brown fox jumps over the lazy dog 1234567890